The Ivory Tower and the Sword

The Ivory Tower and the Sword

Francisco Vitoria Confronts the Emperor

Santiago Piñón Jr.

PICKWICK *Publications* • Eugene, Oregon

THE IVORY TOWER AND THE SWORD
Francisco Vitoria Confronts the Emperor

Pickwick Publications
An Imprint of Wipf and Stock Publishers
199 W. 8th Ave., Suite 3
Eugene, OR 97401

www.wipfandstock.com

PAPERBACK ISBN: 978-1-4982-3578-5
HARDCOVER ISBN: 978-1-4982-3580-8
EBOOK ISBN: 978-1-4982-3579-2

Cataloguing-in-Publication data:

Names: Piñón, Santiago, Jr.

Title: The ivory tower and the sword : Francisco Vitoria confronts the emperor / Santiago Piñón Jr.

Description: Eugene, OR: Pickwick Publications, 2016 | Includes bibliographical references and index.

Identifiers: ISBN 978-1-4982-3578-5 (paperback) | ISBN 978-1-4982-3580-8 (hardcover) | ISBN 978-1-4982-3579-2 (ebook)

Subjects: LSCH: Vitoria, Francisco de, 1486?–1546. | Vitoria, Francisco de, 1486?–1546—Political and social views. | Latin America—History—To 1600. | Latin America—Colonization.

Classification: BX1749.V58 P56 2016 (paperback)

Manufactured in the U.S.A.   07/06/16

I dedicate this work to the memory of my mother and father, Miguela and Santiago Piñón Sr. Thank you for your support and always believing in me. And, especially to my wife, LizDelia Pinon, who supported me by taking care of our four kids while I stayed at the office and library finishing this manuscript. You are my compass in times of great darkness.

Contents

Introduction

I AM IN AWE of and respect individuals who participate in public protests for the sake of standing on the side of justice. Many of my friends took part in the protests held in Ferguson, MO, and other parts of the country. They prepared themselves by gaining support in their endeavors. They marched arm in arm with friends and complete strangers. Often, their participation was nothing more than a peaceful, public display of frustration over the death of Michael Brown, the lack of affordable housing in Oakland, CA, and so forth. However, there were times when their protests were less than peaceful.

My friends have been arrested for keeping true to their convictions. While in Ferguson, MO, and Oakland, CA they were handcuffed, arrested, and taken to jail, where they remained until they could post bail. I stand in amazement at their courage and fearlessness. In a way, I am a little jealous of their arrests because they are invited to various organizations to speak about their experience of being arrested for their convictions. As they speak about standing besides hundreds of others who were also protesting, and talk about their arrests as badges of honor, I cower in the shadows for fear that someone will turn to me and ask what I have done for the sake of justice. I have never been arrested. The only times I have seen the inside of a jail or prison cell were moments when I knew that I would be getting out as soon as our prison ministry trip or Bible study concluded. I have never had to wait for bail to be posted before getting out of jail. The longest I waited was the time it took the prison guard to find my belongings as I returned to the van that was waiting to take us back to the church building where we would get in our own vehicles and make our way home. I have no arrests as badges of honor. Yet I too am just as interested in justice as my friends who have worn the shakles of protest. How, then, do I stand for justice without the fear of being arrested? Are there examples of individuals who stood for justice, but did so without getting arrested or jailed?

Francisco Vitoria is a well-known figure to those outside the disciplines of religion and theology. For example, Hugo Grotius extracted from Vitoria's writings insights to develop his modern notion of international law.[1] James Brown Scott, professor of International Law, argues that the Spanish theorists associated with the Salamancan school were the true founders of International Law.[2] Harold J. Berman, in his *Law and Revolution II*, argues that Vitoria's writings became foundational for later Protestant jurists.[3] Concerning human rights, Brian Tierney considers Vitoria as one of the major voices from the School of Salamanca to argue for the necessary relationship between "individual and community."[4] A student of sixteenth-century Spain would find great encouragement from the scholars mentioned above. However, the general public may have never heard of Vitoria. In fact, they may be more familiar with his contemporary Bartolomé de las Casas.

Of course, Las Casas is the great "Defender of the Indians" who worked tirelessly for the fair and just treatment of the Indians in the New World and to defend them from the Spaniards. Many are attracted to him for his bold and unapologetic critique of the conquistadores who Las Casas portrayed as ruthless, merciless, callous, and cruel in their treatment of the natives. By contrast, Vitoria never travelled to the New World, but rather heard reports of the cruel treatments of the natives. He never published any works during his lifetime, and the texts we have of his today are class notes gathered by his students. We are thankful that he practiced the art of *dictatio*—lecturing at a pace that allows students to take notes verbatim, and that, not being polemical like Las Casas, he is calm, collected, and rational in his texts. At the same time, Vitoria's clarity and forcefulness resulted in Charles V asksing the University Chancellor to reign in individuals who were speaking against the common good of the Crown. Everyone knew that Charles V had Francisco Vitoria in mind. Much more will be said concerning this exchange. For now it is enough to recognize that Vitoria was

---

1. Grotius, *Of the Rights of War and Peace*.
2. Scott, *The Spanish Origin*.
3. Berman, *Law and Revolution II*, 60.
4. Tierney, *Idea of Natural Rights*, 8–9.

able to exert great influence concerning justice from his place in the ivory tower.

This book will demonstrate that Vitoria was a scholastic theologian who incorporated and used humanistic ideas, such as stylistic methods that compel behavioral changes and allow Vitoria to address social concerns regarding law and human dignity, all within the confines of his ivory tower. In doing so, I contend that Vitoria was just as interested in justice as Las Casas. Vitoria adopted humanistic approaches, such as the desire to change the hearts of individuals, a common humanistic concern, which provided him with a substantive and realistic view of the contemporary political state of affairs. Together with his scholastic method, this gave him a theological foundation that allowed him to address contemporary social concerns such as those addressed in his *relecciones*, including *De Los Indios*, which is where Vitoria develops his idea of *ius gentium*. *De Los Indios* provides a humanistic account of Vitoria's theology and conception of law that elucidates the inner coherence of his own work, counters false readings of his work, and opens up constructive possibilities. Unless one keeps in mind both humanistic and scholastic influences in his writings one will fail to grasp the full force of the arguments that Vitoria makes. In addressing contemporary social ills, a theologian must be aware of and glean from other disciplines and allow his theology to engage these disciplines so that they inform one another. This interdisciplinary approach is suitable because it addresses the many aspects of the human being. In addition to being spiritual, the human being is also political, social, and communal. A theological approach that fails to take into account the human being as a whole falls short of being relevant.

It is possible to have an influence in society without having to participate in every worthwhile protest. It is possible to exercise one's mind from behind a desk and in front of a computer and have some kind of influence concerning social justice. This book seeks to highlight Vitoria as an example for doing constructive theology that invokes a discourse across disciplines —such as, among others, theology, politics, and law. It explores Francisco Vitoria's use of rhetoric, both as a style and as a philosophy, which addresses the legal problem of Spain's presence in the New World. Following the lead of humanists during his time period, Vitoria maintained that one could move the will of people to act morally through rhetoric. He specifically has in mind persuading the Holy Roman Emperor to act justly toward the natives. In terms of law, Vitoria develops the notion of *ius gentium*, law of nations, to convince the Emperor to align himself with laws that are just in their application to all people. In short, he subjects the coercive power to a law and community, and simultaneously includes those who had previously been excluded in a world community that has natural rights based on nature rather than divine right. The difficulty facing Vitoria is the coercive power that could endanger his life. Therefore, he employs a rhetorical device called safe-criticism that allows his students and audience—including the Emperor—to reach conclusions on their own. These conclusions, however, Vitoria directs by setting up the postulates and propositions that will guide their rational thinking. Law becomes the means for persuading a human being to act morally.

The first chapter, "Law, Conquest, and the New World," considers the legal and religious justifications for the Spanish conquest of the New World. It seeks to situate Vitoria's concerns in the sixteenth century, a context involving the cruel treatment of natives. This chapter is especially important because it brings to the foreground the importance that law played in the conquest. Rather than exerting its military force and power, Spain justifies its actions in the New World on the basis of law. By considering the legal ramifications of the conquest, it is possible to gain insight into Vitoria's appeal to *ius gentium*—the law of nations. For an empire that is overly concerned with the legal legitimacy of its actions, the introduction of another legal framework—i.e., the law of nations—forces those who claim to abide by law to reassess their previous stance in light of another law that is presented as being above human law—the law of the empire.

Chapter 2, "Political Prudence and a World Community," is a reflection on how Vitoria employs both humanism and scholasticism to call into question the emperor's role in the New World. This chapter provides a close reading of Vitoria's work on the notion of *ius gentium*, or the law of nations. Here we will take note of the issues that are addressed by Vitoria that influences the use of rhetoric. One such issue is that he develops the notion of the law of nations, which results in Vitoria holding the emperor accountable to a higher law.

Chapter 3, "Restraining Power in War," situates Vitoria within a history of just-war theory. By reflecting on various thinkers that have influenced Vitoria, it is possible to take into account how he interacts with these thinkers and moves beyond them in developing his own view of just war. At issue in this chapter is not Vitoria's specific position on war. Instead, it considers his approach to the inquiry of war. That he raises the question of the justice of Spain's presence in the New World is reflective of the human-istic branch that considers rhetoric as a philosophy that takes into account the moral character of people.

The fourth chapter, "Theology, Authority, and Coercion," suggests possibilities for Francisco Vitoria's use of a rhetorical approach in those *relecciónes* that concern the emperor of Spain. Here I make frequent com-parisons to Las Casas because he is representative of the standard and canon for Latino/a Theology, which I argue must be widened to include Francisco Vitoria; unlike Las Casas he is seeking justice from inside an empire.

The final chapter, "Spain, Humanism, and Vitoria," sets in context the humanistic-scholastic debate leading up to the sixteenth century noting on the one hand that humanists are reacting to the dialectical systematic approach of the scholastics by arguing that they are unconcerned with the moral life of the individual, and on the other that scholastics responded to the humanists by arguing that they are uninterested in truth and are nothing more than charlatans. Vitoria pulls this dichotomy together by ad-dressing the moral life while searching for truth. He adopts what Ernesto Grassi calls a philosophical rhetoric. This rhetorical approach allows the reader to draw conclusions without the author having to specifically men-tion the conclusions that ought to be drawn. This approach was used when the author was addressing a ruler who had the power to take the reader's life. Finally, like many orators, the authors would not specifically state that he is using a particular rhetorical style. This chapter closes by considering Vitoria's humanistic training as a student at the University of Paris and the humanism that was present at the Universidad de Salamanca while Vitoria held his chair in theology.

This book is first and foremost an attempt at retrieving for Christian theology an important scholastic theologian who is interested in the inter-relationship between theology and politics. Second, it clarifies the terrain of constructive theology by upholding the dialogue that ought to be taking place between theology, political attentiveness, and the legal discipline. It seeks to open up new levels of constructive thought for issues concerning justice, especially for those who are prone to avoid public protests. Third, it considers how a scholastic approach to theology, i.e., a neo-scholasticism as developed by Vitoria, addresses humanist and political concerns. Fourth, it seeks to provide a new reading of post-colonial thought, specifically of the minds that are supposedly behind the colonial atrocities.

Acknowledgments

AS WITH ANY PROJECT, this book is the result of many people who have played an important supportive role. Dr. Kristine Culp, Dean of the Disciples Divinity House of the University of Chicago, so believed in my abilities that she supported me both financially and emotionally. Dr. Garry Sparks, Dr. Spencer Dew, and Chris Dorsey provided valuable critiques in the beginning stages of this project. I am also grateful for the financial support and mentoring that I received from the Hispanic Theological Initiative (HTI). The relationships formed via HTI are too many to mention by name. The dissertation writing group at the University of Chicago, organized by Dr. William Schweiker, the Edward L. Ryerson Distinguished Service Professor of Theological Ethics, proved to be an invaluable resource and offered insight into many of the ideas that are part of this book. Dr. Schweiker always pushed me in ways that made me believe in myself. Dr. Winnifred Fallers Sullivan, Professor and Chair of the Department of Religious Studies at Indiana University Bloomington, will always have a special place in my life as her advice kept me from quitting the doctorate program after my father's death. I am also thankful for Dr. Susan Schreiner, Professor of the History of Christianity and Theology, for her encouragement and valuable insight into important debates in sixteenth-century Spain. I am especially grateful for my colleagues in the Religion Department of Texas Christian University, especially those who helped with the indexing: Dr. Nadia Lahutsky, Dr. Scott Langston, Dr. Patricia Duncan, and Dr. Jan Quesada. I would not have been able to stick to the timeline without their help. Finally, the most important person who helped me to complete this project is my wife, Lizdelia. Her constant encouragement to take time to go to the library and to work on this project allowed me to work, even when I did not want to write.

1

Law, Conquest, and the New World

An Appeal to Law

THE WIELDING OF POWER to control land and people has been a key characteristic of all empires, including those organizations that wish to become an empire. From the conquest of the promised land to the Persian empire, the invasion of Alexander the Great to the expanding of Roman borders, the growing sway of the British empire to the rise of the colonies in the new world, and now to the modern assault of ISIS, world leaders always offer an explanation for their actions that include the use of power. Conquest must be justified. It is imprudent and unjust to conquer without proper grounds. Spain must be counted among those who exercised power and wished to expand their borders in hope of establishing its empire. Of the many charges that could be brought against Spain, the dismissal of law would not be among them. Spain was especially interested in abiding by the rule of law in all of its endeavors. For instance, the *requerimiento* required the natives to respond to the preaching of the gospel and accept the authority of the Church. If the natives rejected said preaching, then the Spaniards were, they reasoned, justified in attacking and killing the natives. Though there were many in Spain who argued this was an absurd attempt to get the natives to deny their natural rights to property, it still demonstrates a concern for lawfulness. Among those who complained was the renowned Bartolomé de Las Casas, who believed this legal maneuvering was simply for the conquerors to appear to be legally justified in their treatment of the natives.

This judgment is shared by many individuals in the postcolonial camp who conclude that Spain used law to justify their conquest of the new world. Yet, law may not only be used to justify conquest; it can also be used to hold accountable for their actions those who have authority.

If Spain considers its treatment of the natives justifiable under law, then that same legal code can be used to restrain cruel actions. Moreover, it is possible that others may call into question the legality of the actions that were justified. Such is the outlook of Francisco Vitoria, who thinks that Lopez de Palacios's reasoning for the *requerimiento* is entirely absurd. One must keep in mind that Vitoria is not simply commenting on a Spanish practice; rather he is critiquing a legal practice that was supported by both the king and queen. As such, he is questioning the Spanish notion of law, or, at the very least, Lopez de Palacios's legal perception.

It is true that Spain conquered the natives of the newly discovered world, and it is equally true that many in its armed forces employed cruel and vicious methods to subjugate the natives. Yet the fact remains that this subjugation did not take place without long and legal deliberation. This fact is often passed over by scholars who—rightly—are quick to condemn the cruel actions of the Spaniards in the New World. Nonetheless, that Spaniards considered it necessary and essential to justify their actions in the New World we will see is of great importance and interest.

This chapter reflects on the religious and legal justification for the Spanish conquest of the New World. I attend primarily to the legal concerns of the conquest rather than the legal means of conquest. I find it more interesting that an entire empire found it necessary to legally justify its expansion than that an existing empire wanted to expand its reach.

At issue is more than simply a different methodological approach: it is a matter of a different view of human nature. Many scholars—including Williams Jr., Rivera-Pagán, and Todorov—consider the conquest of the natives in the New World to have been acts of a vicious empire composed of cruel and violent individuals with little regard for human life. Much of this perspective, I argue, stems from what later came to be called the Black Legend. That Legend regards the Spaniards and the Spanish empire as merciless and ferocious, regardless of the extent of their involvement in the overthrow of the inhabitants in the New World. Benefit of the doubt is rarely given to Spaniards because of the overwhelming accusation that they are bloodthirsty. This reading, however, fails to consider that individuals often desire that which is good. It is appropriate to take a slight detour at this point to define the Black Legend since references to it are found throughout the literature.

Black Legend

The term Black Legend was first used by Julian Juderias in his book *The Black Legend and the Historical Truth* published in 1914.[1] This text has two major aspects. The first focuses on the historical accomplishments that had taken place in Spain in the Middle Ages. The second focuses on the perceptions and attitudes of foreigners toward the Spaniards. Juderias paints such a negative view of Spaniards to establish the preconceived idea that they were cruel and violent.

Thirty years after Juderias's *Black Legend*, Romulo Carbia published his *Historia de la Leyenda Negra Hispanoamericana*.[2] Carbia is mostly concerned with the writings of Bartolomé de Las Casas. Carbia contrasts Las Casas's account of the Spanish cruelties in the New World, as documented in his *The Devastation of the Indies: A Brief Account*, with the eyewitness accounts of the conquest. His conclusion is that the violence that the natives experienced at the hands of the Spaniards was infrequent—whereas Las Casas presents evidence that the cruelty was frequent and brutal.

In addition to considering Las Casas's and eyewitness accounts of the violence in the New World, Carbia also attends to how Spain's enemies, such as those found in England and France, used Las Casas's text as propaganda against the Spaniards.[3] Those who opposed Spain used Las Casas's publication to portray the Spanish as blood-hungry, greedy conquerors who were willing to exterminate an entire civilization to accumulate treasures and riches.[4] This caricature was promoted so as to include not only the actual conquistadores who were in the New World but all of Spain as well. The force of this characterization is that it blinds one to the possibility of recognizing any positive attributes of the Spanish. This is especially so in Todorov's characterization of Spain in his book *The Conquest of America*.[5]

1. Juderias, *Leyenda*.
2. Carbia, *Historia*.
3. Gibson, *Black Legend*.
4. Ibid., 14.
5. Todorov, *Conquest*.

Scholars like Douglas T. Peck have been careful to document the instances where Todorov presents Spain in a negative light to the point that any hints of affirmative statements are absent.[6]

Augustine and the Desire for the Good

In this section I turn to Augustine for two main reasons. First, he provides an ambiguous way of considering empire. Much discussion of empire revolves around the dichotomy of those who have power and those who are unable to exercise it, as well as the common model of center and margin. The difficulty with these models is that there is little fluidity in them. It suggests that one either has power or does not; one is either at the center or at the margins. Yet such rigidity of definition is misleading. There is fluidity or ambiguity in empire. Augustine clearly recognizes this ambiguity when he describes the Roman empire's desire for peace that, however, it achieves through violent means.

The second reason for turning to Augustine is because of my desire to widen the canon that Latina/o theologians reference before the time of Bartolomé de Las Casas. The history of Christian thought is spilling over with resources that could help one address problems and obstacles in the twenty-first century. One such resource is Francisco Vitoria, who also appeals to figures such as Aquinas, Aristotle, Quintilian, Cicero, and Augustine, and in so doing adds to the profundity of Vitoria's arguments. Specifically, I turn to Augustine because he becomes as important a figure as Martin Luther and the Reformation movement. Augustine is also important because Vitoria drew various insights from him to develop his own position on various issues, especially on the topic of Just War.

In his monumental work, the *City of God*, Augustine discusses the purposes of both the city of God and the city of man. Augustine argues that people go to war in pursuit of peace and not simply because they desire war. He writes in chapter 12 of book 19, "Whoever gives even moderate attention to human affairs and to our common nature, will recognize that if there is no man who does not wish to be joyful, neither is there any one who does not wish to have peace." Augustine continues, "It is therefore with the desire for peace that wars are waged, even by those who take pleasure in exercising their warlike nature in command and battle. And hence it is

6. Peck, "Revival," 25–39.

obvious that peace is the end sought for by war."[7] Augustine is careful to distinguish between peace, which is the end that human beings desire, and war, the means to attain peace.

Augustine's insight is that focusing solely on the means of an action overlooks an important aspect of the act: the intention, purpose, or end of the act. It is true that Augustine does not consider the individual who focuses solely on the end of an action as being above reproach. As a matter of fact, when writing about robbers Augustine admits that they are motivated by greed and malice. A robber who is especially powerful will kill his accomplices if he considers them threats. Yet, this same thief will seek peace with those he is unable to kill. As a member of the earthly "city" the robber seeks tranquility in his immediate social order; nonetheless, in this search for peace he also resorts to domination.

In the earthly city, discord is always present—even though the earthly city desires tranquility. The irony is that political entities will often resort to war to bring about tranquility of order. In spite of this irony, Augustine recognizes that the act of war is a political act, and as such it is an act with some good in mind—peace.

The act, the means to the act, and the end of the act are complex. To reduce the Spanish conquest to a simple desire to conquer natives fails to capture the complexity of the conquest and the complexity of the Spaniards' intention. If Spain were only interested in conquering the natives, why would they justify their presence in the new world? I maintain that Spain sought justification for their presence in the new world because they were sincerely interested in justice. Yet, in spite of this desire for justice, like the earthly city, Spain succumbed to the inclinations of human nature when they waged war on the natives. These historical particulars will help illuminate Vitoria's defense of the natives. With this in mind, I turn my attention to the legal record of and justification for the conquest.

Portugal's Claim

To understand Vitoria's legal rhetoric it is necessary to be aware of the legal background that gave occasion to his writings. In 1485 an ecclesiastical commission gathered at the Universidad de Salamanca to discuss Columbus's proposal to search for a western spice route to the Indies.[8] Af-

7. Augustine, *City of God* 19.12 (Dyson, 934).

8. Williams, *American Indian*, 75.

ter this inquiry, another ecclesiastical commission assembled in 1491 and concluded that Columbus's ideas were consistent with the Holy Scriptures. Spain asked for this inquiry because they wanted to avoid Portugal's monopoly in Africa; Columbus's plan for a shorter spice route was attractive to Spain because they were limited by the Papal bulls regarding the extent to which their empire could expand. Portugal controlled the all-important sea port of Lisbon, and the Canary Islands were under papal protection.

In an expedition that took place in 1341, the Canary Islands had been claimed for the Portuguese Crown. Such further explorations and conquests were made possible through the conquest of the African port city of Ceuta, which was also a prominent Muslim gold trade site.[9] The Castilian kingdom continuously challenged Portugal's claim to the "North African coast."[10] This conflict, unsurprisingly, led to an attack on the natives of the Canary Islands, some of whom had already been converted to Christianity. In response to these violent attacks, Pope Eugenius issued a bull in 1434 that banned, "all European Christians from the Canaries as a protective measure for the infidel as well as the converted inhabitants."[11] To say the least, this bull was not favorable to the Portuguese Crown.

In 1436, King Duarte of Portugal appealed the pope's ban. The appeal included a request that the ban be removed so that the Portuguese Crown could continue its conquest on behalf of Christianity. Included in the appeal is a description of the natives who live as uncivilized and irrational barbarians.[12] King Duarte's brother, Henry the Navigator (1394–1460), converted these "barbarians" to Christianity and established laws that "allowed them" to have an ordered civilization. The contrast is apparent. Prior to the arrival of Henry, the natives on the Canary Islands are described in terms of the state of nature.[13] Through Henry's work on the Islands the natives become a civilized society and also accept the Christian faith. Duarte continues his description of the conversion of 400 natives by emphasizing their continued faithfulness in worshipping Christ.[14] Obviously, the missionary work of Prince Henry was successful. Many of the 400 natives who were baptized are still faithful. The only impediment to the advancement of the Gospel,

9. Ibid., 68.

10. Ibid.

11. Ibid.

12. Muldoon, *Expansion*, 69.

13. Ibid., 55.

14. Ibid.

suggests Duarte, may be the pope himself.[15] According to Duarte, the Papal ban is preventing the mission of the church from taking place. The pope, he suggests, ought to take note that his actions are in direct conflict with God.

For his part, the Portuguese king states that the conquest of the Islands was bound to happen and, as such, should be conquered by a kingdom that was inclined to follow papal direction. Furthermore, Duarte states that missionaries would need the protection of the military because the natives were liable to attack them.[16]

Implied in Duarte's comments is an appeal to Pope Innocent IV's (1243–1254) commentary on Innocent III's (1198–1216) *Quod super his* (1209), which insisted that an infidel could not be attacked simply because he was an unbeliever. Innocent IV argues that each individual possesses dominion and is free to select a ruler and have personal property.[17] Both believers and unbelievers have these rights, which the pope cannot deny.[18] Nonetheless, as vicar of Christ the pope has "power not only over Christians but also over all infidels, for Christ had power over all men."[19] So after arguing that all people have dominion, Pope Innocent IV goes on to maintain that the pope has care over both the believer and unbeliever. His rationale for this is that all are part of the flock of Christ. The difference between the believer and unbeliever is that the latter is not part of the sheepfold, and yet conveniently the pope has power not only in the religious but also the political arenas.

Innocent IV argues that the pope has the authority to punish unbelievers who have gone against the law of nature. Innocent IV writes, "I believe that if a gentile, who has no law except the law of nature [to guide him], does something contrary to the law of nature, the pope can lawfully punish him."[20] As vicar of Christ, the pope is able to judge and punish the unbeliever. This authority includes being able to punish Jews who have received leniency from their leaders for moral indiscretion.[21] Papal authority

15. Ibid., 56.

16. Ibid., 54.

17. Ibid., 191. "Men can select rulers for themselves as [the Israelites] selected Saul and many others . . . Sovereignty, possessions, and jurisdiction can exist licitly, without sin, among infidels, as well as among the faithful."

18. Ibid.

19. Ibid.

20. Ibid., 192.

21. Ibid.

is not limited to the unbeliever's rebellion against the law of nature. Instead, Papal power extends to the point of granting indulgences to believers.

"However, the pope can grant indulgences to those who invade the Holy Land for the purpose of recapturing it although the Saracens possess it . . . [but] they possess it illegally," Innocent IV writes. He continues, "and against those infidels who now hold the Holy Land where Christian princes once ruled, the pope can lawfully order and command that [infidel rulers] not molest unjustly the Christians that are their subjects." The sovereignty of the infidels is limited by their treatment of Christians. If an infidel ruler mistreats a Christian, the pope "can deprive them of the jurisdiction and sovereignty they possess over Christians by judicial sentence."[22] Sovereignty is limited by moral imprudence in that the treatment and/or mistreatment of Christians directly affects their right to ownership. While the extent of the pope's power and authority over infidels included granting indulgences to those who fought against the Saracens, Innocent IV is careful to argue that the infidel cannot be forced to convert to Christianity; nor, however, can the infidel prevent the preaching of the gospel.[23]

As Williams mentions, Duarte was aware of the "pope's direct and indirect jurisdiction,"[24] and Duarte was trying to convince Pope Eugenius that he was the most suitable secular power to carry out the papal responsibility of caring for the infidel. As a matter of fact, Duarte had already begun this task, but now wanted to bring it under the oversight and responsibility of the pope. Because Pope Eugenius never responded to Duarte's request, the issue of dominion, at least in practice, remained unresolved. This would become particularly clear with Duarte's descendant.

Romanus Pontifex

In response to Duarte's request through his son Alfonso V (1438–1481), the king of Portugal, Pope Nicholas V, issued the papal bull, *Romanus Pontifex* (1453). Included within the bull is the acknowledgement that infidels possess dominion and, for that reason, an external power cannot wage war against the natives without due cause. However, if infidels are unable to conduct themselves according to natural law, it suggested, the pope has the

---

22. Ibid.

23. Ibid.

24. Ibid., 71.

right, and even the responsibility, of impeding their natural rights.[25] Pope Nicholas V, therefore, gives Alfonso V, king of Portugal, the responsibility of converting the barbarous Canarians. Portugal now has the authority to subjugate and colonize the African nations with the goal of the infidel's conversion.[26]

The *Romanus Pontifex* opens with a brief statement of the pope's mission, which is to bring as many as possible to salvation. The bull states that the pope believes himself to be responsible for the care of the souls of all people.[27] This concern will be transferred to the king of Portugal because he is to be an instrument that assists in the fulfillment of the divine mission. Using atheletic imagery, "Christian missionaries" are to act as champions of the Christian faith and "restrain" those who are considered to be the enemies of Christianity.[28]

Here, the bull specifically has in mind the Moors when it mentions the Saracens. They are to be restrained and put under the dominion of the Christian king, but nothing is mentioned concerning the death of the Saracens. In addition to restraining, the king is given the dual task of defending the Christian faith and bringing others to this same faith. Not only is the king of Portugal to be involved in this mission but so is the *infante* of Portugal.

Along with his nephew King Alfonso, Henry, infant of Portugal, also participated in the mission of the church, and the bull specifically mentions his endeavors. It is these activities that are held up as the ideal of the champion and defender of the Christian faith.[29] Furthermore, it is activities like these that provide the incentive for allowing Portugal to exercise dominance in Africa. Portugal is charged with defending the Christian natives from foreign threats such as those presented by the Saracens.

What is important for the purposes of this study is that access to Africa is dependent on Portugal's care and concern for those who have been converted to the Christian faith. What would happen if the ruler did not act in the best interests of those under his care? Is it possible that the king's legitimate rule in Africa could be questioned if he neglected to serve the well-being of those whom the papacy has given him? While it is uncertain

25. Williams, *American Indian*, 72.

26. Davenport, *European*, 20–26.

27. Ibid., 21.

28. Ibid.

29. Ibid.

what would happen to the king of Portugal if he neglected the newly converted, it is clear that Portugal does have the authority to subdue pagans and nonbelievers into slavery.

Dum Diversas, 1452

When Columbus realized that he had overestimated the amount of gold and silver to be had, he decided to send to Spain the natives who revolted, were captured, and enslaved.[30] Columbus experienced no ethical conflict in enslaving the natives, considering them to be simply another valuable commodity like gold and silver.[31] This notion and act had papal approval and precedent. For by the bull *Dum Diversas* (18 June 1452) Pope Nicholas V had granted Alfonso, king of Portugal, the authority to enslave Saracens and those who were unbelievers. Undoubtedly Columbus would have been nonplussed by the queen's reaction when she asked with what authority Columbus was enslaving the natives—nonplussed because the pope had given Spain the custodial obligation over the natives.[32]

Portugal's treatment of the Africans was the basis for the pope giving them authority over the infidels. A mistreatment of them could result in the annulment of Portugal's rights. It seems that the kings and queens of Portugal and Spain were well aware of the consequences of their actions concerning their subjects. Is Queen Isabella's response evidence that Spain was against slavery? Why would an individual such as Bartolomé de Las Casas suggest that African slaves be used rather than subject the natives to forced labor? Is he unaware of Spain's position? Is Las Casas simply appealing to the *Dum Diversas* bull that allowed the enslavement of non-Christians but not of believers? How is the *encomienda* distinct from slavery?

Spain's Claim: *Inter caetera*, May 3, 1493

Turning attention once again to Spain's request for the *Inter caetera* bulls by Pope Alexander VI, we are now better prepared to understand the context and reasons for Spain's request. Upon his return to Lisbon, the king of Portugal questioned Columbus and informed the "Spanish ambassador that he

---

30. Bakewell, *History*, 71.

31. Williams, *American Indian*, 82.

32. Floyd, *Columbus*, 46–47.

would soon reconnoiter his new western possession, graciously discovered on Lisbon's behalf by the Spanish Crown's agent."[33] Before Columbus could anchor in Spain, the Spanish Crown had already put together a rough copy of *Inter caetera* and had sent it to the pope for papal confirmation that Spain had official title to the newly discovered "Indies."

We see the importance of the Spanish king's request for the *Inter caetera* when he states that the Spanish Crown recognized the authority and jurisdiction that the pope had over the lands of infidels.[34] Spain's haste can also be understood when one considers the fact that Pope Alexander VI (1493–1503) was the Spaniard Rodrigo Borgia, now deeply in debt to the Castilian crown for his ascendancy to the papacy.[35]

Alexander VI immediately responded to Spain's request that it be declared to be the sole possessor of the newly found land by issuing the bulls *Inter caetera* (May 3, 1493), *Eximiae Devotionis* (May 3, 1493), and *Inter caetera* (May 4, 1493). The first two establish the Christian monarch's right of discovery and the right to convert infidels. The last one makes a distinction between the possessions of both Spain and Portugal, and bestows upon Spain title to the newly found lands. I will focus on the third of the three bulls because that one seems to be the most important in terms of jurisdictional matters.

Inter caetera (May 4, 1493) opens with an acknowledgment that the Christian faith is spreading and souls are being added to the kingdom. Along with the spreading of the gospel is the recognition that non-Christian nations are being overthrown, specifically Granada. Alexander VI praises Isabella and Ferdinand for such accomplishments.[36] There is a connection between Spain's previous victory in Granada and its current discovery of land and peoples. The pope states that he is duty-bound to support Spain because of its role in making the gospel known. Not only is the gospel being preached, but individuals are responding and converting to the Christian faith.[37]

With their monotheistic belief system, the newly found natives simply needed someone to instruct them in the Christian faith. As the discoverer of these new lands, Spain is the most obvious mouthpiece for the Christian

33. Williams, *American Indian*, 79.
34. Ibid.
35. Rivera-Pagán, *Violent*, 25.
36. Davenport, *European*, 76.
37. Ibid.

message. An interesting aspect of this bull is its reminder to the king that he is required to obey the pope as if he is one of the apostles.[38] While the king is monarch over the new lands, the pope maintains authority, power, and rule over the king. Papal authority over the king can be gleaned from the fact that the pope states that the bull is issued by his own accord and not in response to a request from the king. The pope emphatically states,

> we, of our own accord, not at your instance nor the request of anyone else in your regard, but of our own sole largess and certain knowledge and out of the fullness of our apostolic power, by the authority of Almighty God conferred upon us in blessed Peter and of the vicarship of Jesus Christ, which we hold on earth.[39]

In light of the fact that Ferdinand's and Isabella's lawyers had put together the *Inter caetera* (May 3, 1493) and submitted it to the pope at Columbus's return, it is also possible to interpret this bull as evidence of Spain making a distinction between themselves and Portugal. Whereas Portugal requested dominion over the Canary Islands and Africa, Spain makes no such request but is nonetheless granted sovereignty due to its victory at Granada and discovery of the New World. There is then an important difference: Spain is granted sovereignty by right of its discovery and not because of a request.

The pope is able to make this grant because, like Innocent IV and Nicholas V, he has authority over the land of infidels. As with the previous bull, the monarch receives from the pope the title to the discovered lands.[40]

To summarize what we have gleaned from Pope Eugenius's and Pope Alexander VI's bulls: First, it is understood that the pope has jurisdiction over the infidels as a divine allowance to ensure that they hear the gospel preached. Second, infidels have divine rights that cannot be disregarded. The only exception is if the infidel conducts her life in such a way that it goes against natural law. Third, in the case of an infidel going against natural law, the Christian monarch has the right to conduct war against the infidel so the latter gives attention to the preaching of the gospel and an ordered society is established. Finally, the fourth aspect we have gleaned is that the monarch has title to the land it has discovered because the pope has granted it said title and because the monarch has acquired the land "by right of discovery." This right of discovery is similar to the "doctrine of

38. Ibid., 77.
39. Ibid.
40. Ibid.

discovery" that Chief Justice John Marshall invoked in the Supreme Court decision in Johnson *v.* M'Intosh (1823), in which decision he concluded that the Indians lived on their lands but did not exercise ownership.

Encomienda

In view of the fact that the pope had granted care of the inhabitants of the New World to Spain it is not surprising that Queen Isabella reacted as she did when she learned that Columbus had enslaved some of the natives. It is equally unsurprising that slavery would cease. What is surprising is that the *encomienda* system was dependent on a master/slave relationship in which the former was granted various natives from which the master could draw for labor, and, in turn, the master would educate the latter in religious truths and protect them from all harm. Normally, the native would serve the master between one and two years. Following Columbus's chastisement, Nicolas de Ovando was appointed as Governor and sought to free all the Indians from Spanish slavery. When Ovando realized that freeing the slaves was detrimental to the task of colonizing the new world, by royal order he reinstated the *encomienda* system.[41] The encomienda is a system of forced labor; it is ostensibly not slavery per se because the Indians would only have to serve for a limited number of years. In practice, the *encomienda* is enslavement because these Indians were rarely, if ever, released from their obligation. Nonetheless, legally it was not slavery. It consisted of a prominent Spaniard who is commended with Indians to serve his purposes.[42] In return the Spaniard would serve the Spanish crown in a military capacity; he would have the obligation of instructing and protecting those natives who were commended to him, and he would provide for the well-being of the clergy.[43]

Requerimiento

One of the most ironic documents of the sixteenth century is the *requerimiento*. This document was "required" to be read to the natives before military action could take place. The reading of the *requerimiento* is

41. Hanke, *Spanish Struggle*, 19–20.

42. Ibid., 19.

43. Williams, *American Indian*, 84.

significant because law is not simply a set of rules or codes, but must also be promulgated, communicated, and explained to those who will be under the precepts of the law.[44] After a narration of creation, the document summarizes the *Inter caetera* bulls, and then requires the inhabitants to acknowledge the Church, the pope, and to accept Ferdinand and Isabella as king and queen. The second requirement is that the natives be willing to hear the gospel preached. If the natives do not satisfy these obligations, then the Spaniards feel justified in commencing to make war against them.[45]

There is some question as to how seriously this document was taken. Both Francisco Vitoria and Bartolomé de Las Casas recognized that the document was absurd. Vitoria, for instance, recognized that the document required the (presumably unwilling) audience to give up dominion that could not be denied. Las Casas also recognized that the document could be grossly misapplied, such as by the common practice of reading the document in Latin in a voice only slightly louder than a whisper.

Francisco Vitoria challenges each of the above points, with the exception of the clause that infidels have dominion that cannot be taken away. His *relecciónes* and *lecturas* must be read in light of the above Papal bulls if one is to comprehend what he seeks to accomplish, i.e., the just treatment of the natives in the New World. Before we are able to turn our attention to Vitoria we must review the occasion for his being concerned with the natives.

From the time that Columbus returned to Spain in 1493 to 1511, there seems to have been not a single individual concerned with how the natives in the New World were being treated. It was not until December of 1511 that the first sermon which condemned the unjust treatment of the natives was preached by the Dominican friar Antonio de Montesinos.[46] The unjust

---

44. Madden, *Political Theory*, 80.

45. Hanke, *Spanish Struggle*, 33.

46. Ibid., 17. "In order to make your sins against the Indians known to you I have come up on this pulpit, I who am a voice of Christ crying in the wilderness of this island, and therefore it behooves you to listen, not with careless attention, but with all your heart and senses, so that you may hear it; for this is going to be the strangest voice that ever you heard, the harshest and hardest and most awful and most dangerous that ever you expected to hear . . . This voice says that you are in mortal sin, that you live and die in it, for the cruelty and tyranny you use in dealing with these innocent people. Tell me, by what right or justice do you keep these Indians in such a cruel and horrible servitude? On what authority have you waged a detestable war against these people, who dwelt quietly and peacefully on their own land? . . . Why do you keep them so oppressed and weary, not giving them enough to eat nor taking care of them in their illness? For with the excessive work you demand of them they fall ill and die, or rather you kill them with

treatment that Montesinos has in mind may be what Las Casas describes in his *The Devastation of the Indies: A Brief Account*. Here, Las Casas describes a horrific event.[47]

Obviously, the cruelty of the Spaniards in the New World was deplorable and inhumane. That the natives suffered under Spanish rule is equally undeniable, yet not all Spaniards supported these practices.

Like Las Casas, some Spaniards argued polemically for the humane treatment of the natives by appealing to a moral sense of right and wrong. Las Casas's text is intended primarily to move his fellow Spaniards to disgust and embarrassment over what their fellow countrymen are doing in the New World. Others, like Montesinos, make legal demands that the cruel treatment of the natives cease. His critique is based on the norm of the *encomienda*, which required Spaniards to protect the natives from all harm. Specifically, he appeals to that which is right and just. Finally, there are some individuals who call into question the cruelties in the New World by appealing both to the moral senses and to what is right and just. Francisco Vitoria falls into this final category. Not only does he appeal to the demands of law but he is also well aware of the moral sensibilities that must be challenged and persuaded.

---

your desire to extract and acquire gold every day. And what care do you take that they should be instructed in religion? . . . Are these not men? Have they not rational souls? Are you not bound to love them as you love yourselves? . . . Be certain that, in such a state as this, you can no more be saved than the Moors or Turks!"

47. Casas, *Devastation*, 127–28. "But now I am going to tell of another action the Spaniards engage in which is perhaps even more ferocious and infernal than the one I have just recounted, and it still goes on at the present time. As has been said, the Spaniards train their fierce dogs to attack, kill and tear to pieces the Indians. It is doubtful that anyone, whether Christian or not, has ever before heard of such a thing as this. The Spaniards keep alive their dogs' appetite for human beings in this way. They have Indians brought to them in chains, then unleash the dogs. The Indians come meekly down the road and are killed. And the Spaniards have butcher shops where the corpses of Indians are hung up, on display, and someone will come in and say, more or less, 'Give me a quarter of that rascal hanging there, to feed my dogs until I can kill another one for them.' As if by a quarter of a hog or other meat . . . Other Spaniards go hunting with their dogs in the mornings and when one of them returns at noon and is asked 'Did you have good hunting?' he will reply, 'Very good! I killed fifteen or twenty rascals and left them with my dogs.'"

Las Siete Partidas

Before concluding this chapter I would like to comment briefly on *Las Siete Partidas*, the legal code ordered by King Alfonso X, the Castilian king (1252–1284). While this chapter deals primarily with documents that led to the conquest of the natives in the New World, it is important to consider this additional document that was influential in calling into question the cruel practices of the Spaniards. When Montesinos, Las Casas, and Vitoria begin to question the cruel practices in the New World and appeal to law for support, they are, in fact, following a long tradition that can be traced back to the kingdom of Castile in the thirteenth century.

Despite the fact that *Las Siete Partidas* came into existence in the thirteenth century, they were not implemented until the sixteenth century.[48] The most interesting sections for our purposes are the sections that consider slavery. Before examining these it is prudent to consider the trend of the debate over slavery in the sixteenth century. This contested issue came to a head with the debate between Sepulveda and Las Casas. At stake is the nature of the natives in the New World—are they slaves or are they human beings created in the image of God?

Queen Isabella severely reproached Columbus when he presented her with slaves. Yet, as stated above, Columbus would have been comfortable enslaving the natives. After all, Portuguese practice, with papal approval, allowed the enslavement of peoples they conquered. What then prompted Queen Isabella to react as she did? Some argue that Queen Isabella admonished Columbus because she feared that the pope would disapprove of the enslavement of the natives who had been placed under the care of the Spanish crown. However, why would the pope have disapproved Spanish slavery if Portugal was in the habit of enslaving those it conquered? Surely that practice was commonly accepted and had papal approval? So why would the queen be hesitant to adopt an action that was commonplace? If it was not out of fear of papal disapproval for her actions, then the impetus for her reaction must be something else.

As queen of Castile, Isabella would have been familiar with her predecessors and royal law (*Fuero Real* [1255] and *Las Siete Partidas* [1265]), especially as organized by Ferdinand III (1217–1252), Alfonso X, the Learned (1252–1284), and Alfonso XI (1311–1350). It is true that the *Siete Partidas* failed to "take deep root in actual life, and in general that efforts

---

48. Muldoon, *Expansion*, 87.

of the great kings of the thirteenth and fourteenth centuries to unify the law of Castile succumbed to the pressure of the localities to keep their own customs."[49] Nonetheless, their influence was evident in the colonies of the New World, and continued into the twentieth century. States such as Louisiana, Texas, and California came under direct influence of the *Siete Partidas*. For example, Charles Lobingier, in his introduction to *Las Siete Partidas*, translated by Samuel P. Scott, states that as late as 1924 judges of the Louisiana Supreme Court commented on the Spanish legal text.[50] Moreover, Peggy Liss, author of *Isabel, The Queen* argues that "her sense of justice owed much to his [Alfonso X's] Partidas."[51] How did the *Siete Partidas* gain such influence? A hint may be found in Isabella's restructuring of the Castilian kingdom.

When Isabella was recognized as queen of Castile in 1479, she and her husband, Ferdinand, king of Aragon, sought to unify Spain by limiting the power and influence of the nobility, thereby increasing the power of the Crown. This move should come as no surprise, especially when one considers that the major obstacle to the promulgation of the *Siete Partidas* of Alfonso X was the resistance of the particular localities that wanted to keep their own customs. With the decrease of noble power, the Spanish Crown was able to establish itself as the means to unity. Moreover, the *Siete Partidas* could be used as the unifying adhesive that failed in the thirteenth century, but with the weakened nobility in the fifteenth century, the legal code of Alfonso X could be used rather than coordinating a new set of laws.

Queen Isabella had been directly influenced by the *Siete Partidas*. Seeking to educate her son in the tradition of the mirror of princes, she followed principles found in the *Siete Partidas*.[52] Some of these principles were directed to the Divine in terms of having the proper knowledge, love, fear, and service of God. Other principles addressed virtues toward one's fellow human beings.[53] Of course, modifications were made, but the principles were applied to her kingdom; she also oversaw the organizing and publication of the code that would be available in print form in 1495.[54] The influence of the *Siete Partidas* can especially be seen by the concord that existed

49. Berman, *Law and Revolution*, 513.

50. Scott et al., *Siete Partidas*, xii.

51. Liss, *Isabel*, 150.

52. Ibid., 252.

53. Scott et al., *Las Siete Partidas*, vol. 1.

54. Nervo, *Isabella*, 114–15.

between Queen Isabella and King Ferdinand; the *Siete Partidas* describes an ideal and harmonious relationship between the king and queen.[55] Nevertheless, the strongest evidence that she did possess some knowledge of Alfonso X's laws is found when one considers her reaction to Columbus enslaving the natives. Had Isabella adopted Portugal's practice of conquest, then slavery would have been an obvious option. However, her surprise reaction to the enslavement of the natives may be due to the fact that the *Siete Partidas* recognizes that slavery is part of everyday life, nevertheless, it attempted to alleviate such a practice.

In Title V of the *Siete Partidas*, slavery is recognized as a despicable act. "Servitude is," reads Title V, "the vilest and most contemptible thing that can exist among men."[56] Immediately, one realizes that slavery is viewed as not being natural, as with Aristotle. Instead, slavery is the result of one individual exercising power over another. The individual who becomes enslaved does so because he "is brought by means of it under the power of another, so that the latter can do with him what he pleases, just as he can with any of the rest of his property living or dead."[57] Again, slavery is not an assigned role that fate gives, nor is it ordained by God.

According to the code, Title XXI, Law One, there are three ways that an individual can become a slave.[58] A human being can become a slave as a result of war. One can be born a slave if one's mother is a slave. Finally, an individual can sell himself into slavery. In the first two of these, a person becomes a slave through the power of another, whereas in the third, one sells oneself into slavery.

Because the human being is naturally free and because selling himself into slavery is a negation of his natural being, the legal code is careful to stipulate the requirements for selling oneself into slavery. First, the individual must sell himself into slavery without any outside coercion. Second, the individual who sells himself must be compensated for the sale. Third—and it seems that this is most important—the individual must be aware of his freedom. With this third requirement the code seems to be putting into tension what the individual is doing (selling himself into slavery) and who he is (free). Fourth, the individual who is purchasing the slave must be aware that the one who is selling himself is a slave. With this stipulation the

55. Weissberger, *Queen Isabel*, 8–9.
56. Muldoon, *Expansion*, 88.
57. Ibid.
58. Ibid., 91.

codes seems to be creating an apprehension within the buyer and the seller. The one who is selling himself must realize that he is free and not a slave. The one purchasing must be aware that the individual he is buying is not free, but a slave. In both instances the buyer and seller confront themselves with what they know to be true. It is as if they must convince themselves to go against their beliefs, and to do so requires a negation of their very being. Finally, the code provides an age requirement of twenty years to sell oneself into slavery.[59] The code is careful when discussing the individual selling himself into slavery because this act requires for something to be wrong in the one selling. There must be something wrong because slavery is not a good thing. It is a system of control that makes the slave into nothing more than the owner's property. However, there is tension between the superimposed role of slave and the God-given nature.

In this discussion, the legal code is quick to remind the reader of the nature of the slave. By nature, the slave is, "the most noble and free among all the creatures that God made . . ."[60] There are two characteristics that are especially important for our purposes. The first is that the human being is noble. This suggests that in this human beings are unlike the rest of creation. The second characteristic is the most fascinating because it is in direct conflict with man's position as slave. The human being is free. Freedom here is intended to be in direct contrast with the role of being a slave. Slavery and freedom are in tension in the very being and role of the human being.

I will bring this section on the *Siete Partidas* to a close with a few comments on the relationship between the master and the slave. Concerning this relationship, the code states in Law VI of Title XXI, "A master has complete authority over his slave to dispose of him as he pleases." This statement comes somewhat as a surprise because one would expect nothing else from a master-slave relationship. One expects the master to have complete control over his slave, and for the slave to have no rights. Again, however, the code seems to put the relationship into tension. While the master has authority over the slave, this does not relieve the master from moral responsibilities toward the slave.

According to the code, the master has authority over the body of the slave but not over his life. Under no circumstance is the master to take the life of the slave, or to even cause injury. The master "should not kill or

59. Ibid., 92.
60. Ibid., 91.

wound him, although he may give him cause for it."[61] It is possible that the master may be in the right in desiring the death of the slave or desiring for the slave to be injured. Nevertheless, the master must inquire of a judge as to his right to injure or kill the slave. Death seems not to be an option unless the master finds the slave "with his wife or his daughter, or where he commits some other offence of this sort, for then he certainly has a right to kill him."[62] It is worthy of note that while the master, under specific circumstances, has the right to kill his slave, he must inquire of a judge before he takes any such action.

It is equally interesting to note that the code grants the slave certain rights. If a slave is unable to tolerate the treatment of his master because of starvation or repeated injury, he is able to appeal to the judge. In these cases, the judge has the jurisdiction to take the slave away from the master, sell the slave to another, and give the proceeds to the original master.[63] If this course is taken, then the judge must make certain that the slave "never can be again placed in the power, or under the authority of the party through whose fault they were sold."[64] Even while selling the slave the judge must pay special attention to protect the slave from the previous owner. In other words, the code is aware that a purchaser could turn around and sell the slave back to the original owner. This is what the judge is trying to avoid. The slave, while no longer free, has the legal right not to fear for his life.

In this chapter I have introduced legal and theological texts that suggest that slavery is not an essential category. While these texts acknowledge slavery, they do so without suggesting that a person is a slave by nature. I have also suggested that Queen Isabella's reaction to Columbus's enslavement of the natives might have been due to her being aware of the *Siete Partidas*. Finally, while much of the debate concerning the natives of the New World revolved around whether or not they were barbarians, or rather slaves by nature and Aristotle's categories, Francisco Vitoria argues that the natives are not by nature slaves, without appealing to Aristotle. How was this possible? It is entirely plausible that he knew of the *Siete Partidas* and used them to convince Charles V, heir to Ferdinand's and Isabella's thrones, of acting justly in behalf of the natives by appealing to a document his predecessors acknowledged. At the very least we know that Vitoria is arguing

61. Ibid., 93.
62. Ibid.
63. Ibid.
64. Ibid.

that the natives have certain rights and should not have to be fearful of losing their lives.

The purpose of this chapter was to consider the documents and practices that legitimated the Spanish conquest of the New World. I considered the papal bulls and noted that while Spain was given title over the New World, it was also given the responsibility of sharing the gospel with the inhabitants. Likewise, I reflected on the *encomienda* and *requerimiento* and suggested that there was tension between the Spanish Crown and those Spaniards who were living in the New World. The tension was due to the massive distance between the power of the empire and its subjects.

2

Political Prudence and
a World Community

In this chapter I consider the law of nations as developed and used by Francisco Vitoria in his *relección* titled *On the Indians*. The *relección* was an end-of-the-year event at which professors gave a summary of the lectures they had previously presented in class. Specifically, I consider how Vitoria develops the idea of the law of nations in order to defend the rights of the Indians in the New World. The thesis that Vitoria constructs the law of nations to defend the Indians is at odds with the thesis that the law of nations is an instrument of empire in Spain's conquest of the Americas as defended by scholars such as Luis Rivera-Pagán, author of *A Violent Evangelism: The Political and Religious Conquests of America*,[1] and Robert A. Williams Jr., author of *The American Indian in Western Legal Thought: The Discourses of Conquest*.[2] While it is possible to read Vitoria's *relección* as an instrument of conquest, I argue in this chapter that this is a gross misreading of Vitoria's text and fails to take into consideration the historical data and political conflicts during Vitoria's era.[3]

1. Rivera-Pagán, *Violent.*

2. Williams, *American Indian.*

3. There are several issues that must be considered in another essay and that require more space than is available in this work. One issue to be considered is the use of law by the Spanish conquistadores to justify their presence in the New World. Both Rivera-Pagán and Williams entertain the notion that law was used by Spain in order to have a legal justification for the mistreatment of the natives. While the legal basis for conquest can be understood from a negative perspective in that law allowed the repugnant treatment of entire civilizations, the more interesting aspect of the conquest is the turn to law. If Spain was simply interested in conquering the New World and expanding their empire, then why would they find it necessary to turn to law to justify their actions? It

This chapter of course only explores one aspect of how Vitoria uses theological, juridical, and ethical resources to defend the rights of individuals who are experiencing various kinds of injustices and oppression. I chose the *relección On the Indians* because it is among Vitoria's mature works; *On the Indians or the Spanish Right of War over the Barbarians* is a continuation of the earlier *relección* and further portrays Vitoria's maturity. While the latter *relección* more fully develops the *ius gentium*, I have chosen the earlier one because it is from it that many scholars reach the conclusion that Vitoria was simply interested in justifying Spain's presence in the New World and that his justification of the subjugation of the natives was his chief means of doing so. I, by contrast, would argue that although Vitoria is indeed interested in justifying the presence of Spain in the New World, he is more interested in defending the natives from the cruel persecution they were suffering at the hands of the Spanish. And so, after a brief introduction to Vitoria's life, in this chapter I consider those aspects of *De Los Indios* that best represent Vitoria's objective of defending the rights of Indians. Specifically, I deal with issues that address the rule of Spain and the presence of Spain in the New World. For in appealing to *ius gentium*, Vitoria argues that Spain does not have the right to rule in the New World but that

---

seems that an empire that is interested only in the expansion of its empire would find law as an obstacle to its goal. Nonetheless, Spain considered law to be such an important component of its society that it made efforts to remain within the confines of law. It is true that such an attitude does not necessitate a sincere character on the part of the Spanish empire, but there is some profit to taking Spain at its word. Furthermore, it is Spain's high regard for law that allows individuals such as Las Casas and Vitoria to confront the empire on its own terms.

Another issue that must be considered is the claim offered by both Rivera-Pagán and Williams that, along with law, the Church was also the instrument of conquest. It is argued that the Church's interest in the preaching of the Gospel and the salvation of souls was a means for allowing Spain to expand its borders. While it is impossible to deny the fact that religion was often used to destroy communities, there is some doubt as to whether the evangelistic mind-set was primarily meant to be used as an instrument of empire. Such an outlook calls into question the sincerity of the Church to preach the Good News and its desire to convert people to the Christian faith. Arguments presented by both Las Casas and Vitoria indicate that the Church was sincere in its desire to convert the pagans, and wanted to make sure nothing stood in the way of this conversion, which allowed them to ask the pope to pressure the emperor in changing laws that would protect the natives of the New World. Religion, rather than being solely an instrument of Empire, also serves as an instrument that protects the rights of individuals.

As indicated earlier, the above issues require more time and space than is available in this essay, but will be considered in the wider project. At the moment, it is sufficient to identify alternatives to the views upheld by Rivera-Pagán and Williams.

it does have the right to be present in the New World. Nonetheless, Spain's presence is called into question when Vitoria establishes the conditions of this presence.

Text of *De Los Indios*

Vitoria begins his *relección* by quoting the Great Commission, "Go ye therefore, and teach all nations, baptizing them in the name of the Father, and of the Son, and of the Holy Spirit."[4] The issue that Vitoria raises is more than a consideration of the right and authority of the church to baptize the children of unbelievers against the will of the parents. At first sight it would appear that Vitoria is interested in the authority of the church to subvert the authority of non-believing parents. With a little more scrutiny it becomes clear that actually Vitoria is concerned with the notion of dominion and authority of the natives of the New World.

In chapter 4 I will brief consider the notion of dominion as it was addressed by the Council of Constance and recounted in the writings of Wycliffe, who argued that dominion was dependent on the moral worthiness of the individual. If an individual fell out of God's favor, then dominion was relinquished. Such a position allowed rulers to dispossess clerics of their possessions.

It is equally important to recall that in his initial *relección* Vitoria, going against the prevailing Catholic thought of his day, would argue that dominion is based on divine right. Later, he would change his position in his *relección* that addressed ecclesial power. While one may wish that he had given an explanation for this change, we are left to contend with an earlier Vitoria and a more mature theologian. In the present consideration of *On the Indians*, we must acknowledge that we are dealing with Vitoria's most mature thought on the subject of dominion and authority. This *relección* shows Vitoria dealing with prevailing authority figures such as Peter Lombard and Thomas Aquinas, who was beginning to rise in importance, and his own thought. Vitoria, following Lombard and Aquinas, will argue that the natives of the New World have dominion that cannot be disparaged by the authority of the church.

According to Thomas Aquinas, it is an injustice to baptize the children of unbelievers because this eliminates parental authority, i.e., dominion,

4. Vitoria, *Obras*, 233.

that parents have over their children.[5] This authority is given to the parents by natural law, and nothing ought to remove that authority. Parents, therefore, have dominion over their children. As a Thomistic scholar, Vitoria is aware of Aquinas's conclusion and of the church's practice, and yet he uses the issue of parental authority to address the rights of the natives in the New World, specifically the question, do the Indians possess dominion? If a parent in the New World is able to keep the Church from baptizing her child because of the authority and dominion she has, then the authority of the Church is also limited. Furthermore, if Vitoria is able to prove that the Indians possess dominion, then he will call into question the power that Spain is exercising in the New World.

Rule vs. Presence in the New World

According to Vitoria, the *relección* will contain three parts and will address the following questions: 1. By what right were the barbarians subjected to Spanish rule? 2. What power does the Spanish monarchy have over the Indians in temporal and civil affairs? 3. What power has either the monarchy or the church with regard to the Indians in spiritual and religious matters?[6]

At the outset of the *relección*, following his belief that the theologian ought to be concerned with any and every topic of human concern,[7] Vitoria employs a theological mindset to address a juridical matter.[8] To approach the question of dominion from either a juridical or theological perspective alone implies a perverse understanding of the issue at hand, for neither by itself is able to grasp fully the complexities of the rights of the natives. Furthermore, both theological and juridical approaches are necessary when considering both penal issues and matters of human dignity because each approach focuses on a particular aspect of the human being. The former considers human beings in their relations to the Divine and/or religious

---

5. Aquinas, *Summa*, II–II Q. 10, Art. 12: "Injustice should be done to no man. Now it would be an injustice to Jews if their children were to be baptized against their will, since they would lose the rights of parental authority over their children as soon as these were Christians. Therefore these should not be baptized against their parents' will."

6. Vitoria, *Obras*, 644–43.

7. Vitoria, Pagden, and Lawrance, *Vitoria*, 3. Vitoria writes, "The office and calling of a theologian is so wide, that no argument or controversy on any subject can be considered foreign to his profession."

8. Scott, *Spanish Origin*, 98.

institutions that oftentimes influence penal institutions. By its coercive nature, the latter affects the individual's body which could undermine any kind of dignity that is present.

Recognizing that he would be confronting both the emperor and the pope, Vitoria considers the justification for raising the question of the Indians' dominion. First, he takes into account the power of the Spanish empire by admitting that the Spanish Crown indeed possesses the New World. Second, Vitoria recounts the titles of Ferdinand and Isabella as "Most Christian" and Carlos V as "Most righteous and just emperor"[9]—the former being the monarchs who first occupied the New World, and the latter being the current ruling emperor who occupies the New World. Vitoria gives the above rulers the benefit of the doubt that they actually considered whether or not they have the right to rule the New World. This justification is especially important because if doubt should happen to arise, then the question of the Spanish Crown's right to rule in the New World is necessarily made central. It is this very doubt and question that Vitoria himself raises.

At the onset of *On the Indians*, Vitoria mentions the primary evidence for considering the illegal subjection of the natives by the Spanish Crown.[10] Though Vitoria is mostly concerned with the justification of Spanish presence in the New World, he is also very concerned with the cruelty that the natives are experiencing. The rumors of Spanish cruelty are always on his mind, even when he is writing on matters that have little to do with the New World. Much of his distress over the treatment of the Indians may be found in his personal letters. These will be considered at a different time. What is important to note here is that the ill treatment of the natives is what, for Vitoria, raises the issue of justice.

There are, therefore, two facts that must be remembered as one reads *De Los Indios*. First, Vitoria is uncertain of the legitimacy of the natives' subjection to the Spanish Crown. Second, Vitoria has constantly before his eyes the cruelties that the natives are experiencing. With these thoughts, we move to the former matter and consider Vitoria's position concerning the Spanish presence in the New World.

Surprisingly, Vitoria concludes the introduction to *On the Indians* by stating that the Indians are not subject to the Spanish Crown, according to human law, and as such, the issue of the presence of Spain in the New

---

9. Vitoria, *Obras*, 643.

10. Ibid., 648; Vitoria, Pagden, and Lawrance, *Vitoria*, 238.

World requires a theological perspective on the case of the natives because theologians are able to offer a different perspective to cases of conscience.[11]

Vitoria considers subjection of the Indians to the Spanish Crown in detail when he considers the titles by which Spain claimed dominion. Again, following the scholastic method, Vitoria presents evidence that legitimates Spanish dominion, evidence that revolves around the natives' right to ownership. The notion of ownership is considered because according to Aristotle and Justinian's *Institutes* and *Digest*, a slave had no right to own anything of his own. Spanish dominion was based either on the belief that the natives were slaves by nature (thus giving Spain legitimate dominion because if a master abandoned a slave, then any one else could take possession of the abandoned slave); or Spanish dominion was validated on account of the natives' unbelief: their unbelief prohibited them from the right to ownership, which consequently allowed the Spanish faithful to exercise dominion in the New World.

In response to the above notions, Vitoria appeals to Thomas Aquinas who argued that unbelief does not rule out ownership.[12] In addition to appealing to Aquinas, Vitoria turns to both the Holy Scriptures (Rom 13:1–5; 1 Pet 2:13–14) and to reason to prove his point that the natives have not forfeited their right to ownership because of their unbelief. In fact, Vitoria argues, the natives exercised ownership prior to the arrival of the Spanish Crown in the New World, thus giving the Indians the right of accession of possession, an argument that is found in both Justinian's *Institutes* 44.3.2 and *Digest* 11.19.7.

Vitoria's argument is fourfold: First, he appeals to the greatest theologian of his order, the Dominican Thomas Aquinas, whose influence and respect were advanced by Vitoria as we see from the fact that he taught from the *Summa* rather than the *Sentences*. Second, Vitoria turns his attention to the Scriptures that are honored and venerated throughout the entire church. An appeal to reason is the third component of Vitoria's argument. Here, referring to Aquinas, Vitoria states that unbelief does not cancel out either human law or natural law. The fourth is an appeal to the historical fact that the Indians in fact had many possessions, which means they already had and exercised some form of dominion. To establish the dominion of the natives, Vitoria will appeal to Justinian.

11. Vitoria, *Obras*, 651.

12. Ibid., 656.

When taken alone, each of these arguments seems to stand in opposition to the arguments of Vitoria's antagonists. His antagonists appealed to Aristotle; Vitoria appeals to one of the greatest interpreters of Aristotle—Thomas Aquinas. Both Vitoria and his antagonists appeal to Scripture, but Vitoria uses biblical texts that defend the dominion of unbelievers. Vitoria and the antagonists appeal to reason with the former appealing to Aquinas, human and natural law, while the latter have argued that the Indians are slaves by nature. Both the antagonists and Vitoria appeal to historical facts. The former appeals to the fact that the Spanish Crown is in possession of natives, the latter argues that the natives exercised dominion prior to the arrival of the Spanish in the New World. Finally, both the antagonists and Vitoria have appealed to Roman law—Justinian's *Institutes* and the *Digest*.

The strength of Vitoria's argument is found in the overall structure of the argument. While each individual aspect of his argument is stronger than his opponents', it is the argument as a whole that makes the greatest impact. The natives have dominion because they exercised dominion prior to the arrival of the Spanish Crown, and Scripture, reason, Roman law, and historical fact testify to this fact of the Indians' dominion.

The Rule of Spain in the New World

Here we begin to see how the law of nations is taking shape. Vitoria has established that the Indians exercised ownership, a right that is defended in Roman law. If Roman law can be shown to be applicable to the natives, then Vitoria can also argue that Roman law, through the law of nations, can be used to defend the rights of natives and to hold Spain accountable for its actions in the New World. The most important step to holding Spain accountable is demonstrating that the natives exercised ownership prior to the arrival of the Spanish Crown in the New World. If it is true that the Indians exercised ownership, then one must reconsider the basis for Spain's legitimate dominion in the New World, which is exactly what Vitoria does in the following section of *On the Indians*.

Having established the natives' exercise of ownership, Vitoria turns his attention to the titles by which the New World could have passed to Spain. At issue here is the right by which Spain is able to claim a legitimate right to be in the New World. While Vitoria presents seven illegitimate titles by which the natives could have been made subject to Spain, I will mention only those that are relevant to Vitoria's use of the law of nations to defend the natives from the cruel ill-treatment that the Spanish Crown was inflicting.

The first illegitimate title that Vitoria considers is a clear indication of why this document was prohibited from being published immediately after being delivered. Vitoria, after considering various positions for the Spanish emperor to be thought of as master of the entire world—an argument that Vitoria's antagonists used to defend the legitimacy of Spanish rule in the New World—he responds in a direct and explicit manner: "The emperor is not master of the entire world."[13] The emperor's dominion over natives can be established, Vitoria argues, in three ways: by natural law, divine law, and human law.[14] Yet, dominion of a single emperor has not been established by any of the above notions. Natural law establishes parental dominion over children (and, unfortunately, Vitoria also argues that husbands have dominion over their wives); such dominion, however, is not transferred to rulers. Therefore, natural law does not establish the dominion of the emperor.

Likewise divine law establishes the rule of Christ over the entire world, and not the rule of the emperor over the world.[15] Vitoria demonstrates from the biblical text that individuals such as Saul, David, Noah, Abraham, and Lot exercised dominion over a particular land; this rule, rather than being given by divine lot, is passed on from one individual to another through inheritance. Therefore, divine law also, like natural law, does not establish the dominion of the emperor over the entire world.

Human law could establish the rule of the emperor over the entire world if there were an enactment, but such an enactment does not exist. In order to be clearly understood, Vitoria becomes almost redundant with his argument that the emperor does not have any rule over the whole world. Vitoria writes, "Nor does the emperor have universal dominion by legitimate succession, gift, exchange, purchase, just war, election, or any other legal title, as is established. Therefore the emperor has never been master of the whole world."[16] By arguing from natural, divine, and human law that the Spanish Crown has no rule over the natives in the New World, Vitoria has attacked every conceivable legal justification for Spanish rule.

13. Ibid., 669.

14. Ibid.

15. Ibid., 670.

16. Ibid., 675; Vitoria, Pagden, and Lawrance, *Vitoria*, 257–58.

Arguments that maintain that Vitoria never questioned the legitimacy of Spanish dominion are simply absurd.[17]

The force of Vitoria's argument is reflected in Carlos V's reaction to the reading. On November 10, 1539, Carlos V wrote to the prior of the Dominican faculty calling for the end of any discussion questioning the legitimacy of Spanish rule in the New World.[18] According to Rivera-Pagán, the emperor responded to the independent discussions that were taking place at the Universidad de Salamanca, rather than to Vitoria's specific lecture. The basis for Rivera-Pagán's argument is that Carlos V would later ask Vitoria to be a Spanish delegate to the Council of Trent. Rivera-Pagán assumes that this request implies an amicable relationship between Vitoria and Carlos V.

Yet Rivera-Pagán's reading of the emperor's request that one interpret Vitoria's case—that Carlos V is not emperor of the entire world—in a different manner is impossible if one is going to be fair to Vitoria's words. Also, Rivera-Pagán's assumption of an amicable relationship between Vitoria and Carlos V fails to grasp the many fronts on which Carlos V was fighting in the sixteenth century.

The request for Vitoria to serve as a delegate demonstrates, if nothing else, the complex relationship that Carlos V had with the Dominicans. On the one hand, the Dominicans, such as Vitoria and Las Casas, were questioning the rule of the Spanish Crown in the New World and were a sore spot for Carlos V. On the other hand, however, it was the Dominicans who were best equipped to confront the challenges of the Reformation. If nothing else, the Dominicans represented the enemies of Carlos V's enemies, the Protestants, and so they would then prove to be his friends when it came time to confront the Reformation.

After leveling his attack against the Spanish emperor's rule of the Indies, Vitoria turns his attention to the pope, the other authority figure that legitimized the maltreatment of the Indians. A second title that could legitimize Spanish rule in the New World is "the Pope is monarch of the whole world, even in temporal matters, and consequently that he was empowered to constitute the kings of Spain as kings, lords of those lands."[19] Following a plethora of witnesses who testify to the pope's authority to make the Spanish emperor lord of the New World, Vitoria states that the basis for their

17. Such is Rivera-Pagán's position. Cf. *Violent*, 83, 84.

18. Quoted in Rivera-Pagán, *Violent*, 84.

19. Vitoria, *Obras*, 676; Vitoria, Pagden, and Lawrance, *Vitoria*, 258.

views is based on two biblical texts (Ps 24:1; Matt 28:18), which are taken out of context and misunderstood.

My analysis of Vitoria's position concerning the authority of the pope will be considered more fully when I analyze his text *On the Power of Church*. It is enough at this point to state that Vitoria's argument against the pope authorizing Spanish rule is that the pope lacks authority over unbelievers.[20] Also, according to Vitoria, if the pope had secular authority over the world, then the pope could not transfer his authority to other secular rulers because this would imply that the pope was relinquishing his authority, which is something he could never do.[21]

A third unjust title by which the Spanish emperor could possess the New World is through the right of discovery. Vitoria states that the right of discovery was in force at the time that Columbus set sail, thus giving Spain ownership of the New World. As understood by Vitoria, the authority of the right of discovery is found in Justinian's *Institutes* 2.1.12, which states, "Where something has no owner, it is reasonable that the person who takes it should have it."[22] In defense of the Indians, Vitoria responds by stating that the law of nations, referring to the above legal text, states that goods are transferred to an owner only in the case when the goods clearly had no owner. This, of course, cannot be applied to the natives of the New World because Vitoria has already proven that the Indians exercised private and public dominion. Rather than using it against the Indians, Vitoria uses the law of nations to argue that Spain has no title to the New World.

While this is Vitoria's shortest consideration of an unjust title, it contains several hints as to how he will use the law of nations in defense of the Indians. First, the law of nations is a notion that is applicable to contemporary situations. It is not a law that remains in the past, but rather one that can be used to hold empires accountable in the present. Second, Vitoria expects empires such as Spain to recognize and submit to the law of nations. Finally, the law of nations is a law that is concerned with justice, for both Spain and the natives. In other words, to be effective the law of nations must recognize the legal rights of all parties involved and cannot be applied to give preferential treatment to any single party. This will be especially evident when we turn our attention to the final section of *De Los Indios*.

---

20. Vitoria, *Obras*, 678.

21. Ibid., 680.

22. Justinian, *Institutes*, 2.1.12.

A final unjust title that is worth considering is the fourth title, which allows Spain to exercise dominion in the New World because of the natives' refusal to accept the Christian faith despite unrelenting preaching—"they refuse to accept the faith of Christ, although they have been acquainted with and exhorted with insistent requests to accept it."[23] A rejection of the Christian faith, according to Vitoria's antagonists, entails blaspheming Christ. War is the means for controlling and quenching blasphemy.

Among his many defenses, Vitoria replies by stating that he doubts that "the Christian faith has been presented and announced in such a way that the barbarians would be obligated to believe under new sin."[24] Vitoria maintains that no one is bound to believe the Christian faith without "probable motives of persuasion," which entail miracles, signs, and "religious examples of life."[25] The cruel treatments that the Spaniards have been imposing on the natives, which Vitoria calls "sinful acts," become obstacles to those individuals who are sincerely trying to preach the gospel.

Vitoria concludes his commentary on the fourth unjust title by stating that the rejection of the gospel by the natives does not necessitate war. War, therefore, cannot be justified on the basis that others have rejected the Christian faith because conversion entails freedom of will, and war, through fear, eliminates free choice.

We have therefore considered Vitoria's attack on both the Spanish emperor and the Catholic pope by insisting that Carlos V does not have dominion over the New World, and that the pope cannot give the New World to the emperor. Vitoria has appealed to the law of nations to demonstrate that the Indians possessed dominion prior to the Spaniards' arrival in the New World, and, as such, Spain cannot claim the dominion by right of discovery. Vitoria shows that from every conceivable perspective the Spanish empire has no right to exercise dominion in the New World and rule the natives. However, the question that begs to be asked is whether or not Spain even has the right to be in the New World. This, of course, is an entirely different question from whether Spain ought to have dominion over the New World.

23. Vitoria, *Obras*, 685.
24. Ibid., 695.
25. Ibid.

The Presence of Spain
in the New World

The third section of *On the Indians* marks Vitoria's innovativeness in his search for justice and life for the natives of the New World. While there are many elements in this section that serve as an impetus for many debates—such as what other scholars claim about Vitoria allowing imperial domination by giving the Catholic Church too much authority in terms of defending the common good for converts in the New World, which would allow continued Spanish imperial rule—I will continue my focus on Vitoria's development and use of *ius gentium*.

The third section begins with the issue that was raised above, i.e., whether or not Spain has the right to be in the New World. Briefly put, Vitoria contends that Spain can travel in the New World, but he includes in his assertions conditional elements that are almost impossible for the Spanish empire to meet. These in turn force one to entertain the question of whether Vitoria actually believed that the Spanish empire ought to be in the New World.

Vitoria begins the third section by writing, "The Spaniards have the right to travel and remain in their provinces, without the barbarians prohibiting them, as long as they do no harm."[26] Vitoria claims that all nations have an equal obligation to treat foreigners with kindness. The most interesting aspect of Vitoria's argument is that he assumes that all nations abide with the kind treatment of foreigners. In this assumption Vitoria fails to appeal specifically to Roman law for his argument. In other words, Vitoria seems to be involved in creating a law to which all nations would adhere. Yet, it is this very law that gives the Spaniards the right to travel in the New World and also places conditions upon their travels.

Vitoria will appeal to a specific Roman law when he argues that the Spaniards have the right to use the riverbanks of the New World. According to the *Institutes*, all people have the right to use the rivers and put in on the banks because these banks are considered public property thereby giving all people access.[27] The land, in contrast to the river, may have a specific owner, but this ownership does not entail the right to bar others from the banks of the river.[28] For Vitoria, then, it is conceivable for the natives to

---

26. Ibid., 705.

27. Justinian, *Institutes*, 55.

28. Ibid. "But ownership of the banks is vested in the adjacent landowners. That also makes them owners of the trees which grow there" (2:1.4).

allow the Spaniards to use the banks while the Indians maintain ownership of the land.

The Equalizing Effect of *Ius Gentium*

In addition to appealing to *ius gentium* and Roman law, Vitoria appeals to Scripture to establish the Spanish right to travel in the New World. The texts come from Eccl 13:15 [Sirach 13:19], Matt 25:43, Luke 10:29–37, and Matt 22:39, and refer to an amicable relationship that ought to exist between all humankind.[29] While Vitoria specifically mentions these texts to argue that the barbarians ought to allow the Spaniards to travel in the New World, one must consider whether Vitoria intended the Spaniards to recognize how the texts applied to themselves. In short, it seems that even as Vitoria is defending the Spaniards' right to travel he is also defending the natives' right to be treated as equals by the Spanish.

With the addition of Scripture to Roman law and the development of *ius gentium*, Vitoria has established a legal framework that is founded upon both divine law and natural law. Furthermore, it is the appeal to divine and natural law that gives the Spanish the right to insist on the force of law.[30] Without this force of law, Vitoria suggests, that law would not exist. Therefore, force of law requires both a divine and natural legal foundation. While it may appear that the force of law is primarily on the side of the Spaniards—it allows them to travel in the New World and obliges the natives to allow the exercise of this right—the force of law is also applicable to the natives in that they are also to be treated as equals. Not only must the natives treat the Spaniards as equals, but the Spaniards are also bound by the same legal framework to treat the natives as equals. The force of law, therefore, is applicable to both the Spaniards and the natives.

As mentioned, the Spaniards' right to live in the New World is established by the law of nations, which for Vitoria is both natural law and is derived from natural law. Vitoria develops his notion of *ius gentium* from Justinian's *Institutes*, specifically from 1.2.1, which states, "The law of nature is the law instilled by nature in all creatures. It is not merely for mankind but for all creatures of the sky, earth and sea." Furthermore, "the law which natural reason makes for all mankind is applied the same everywhere. It

29. Vitoria, *Obras*, 707.
30. Ibid., 708.

is called 'the law of all peoples' because it is common to every nation. The law of the Roman people is also partly its own and partly common to all mankind."[31] One will notice immediately that the *ius gentium* has both a particular and universal application. Particularly, the Roman law is for the Romans but also applicable to all human beings.

From a brief study of the history of *ius gentium* one finds that *ius gentium* was developed out of the Roman empire's contact with non-Roman citizens. Among Roman citizens, Roman law guided business and religious transactions, but problems arose when non-Roman individuals lived in Roman jurisdictions. How do Roman citizens deal with others who are not under Roman legal obligation when legal obligation is based on an individual's nationality? The solution is found in the development of *ius gentium*, which is applicable to both Roman citizens and foreign citizens.[32]

As was the case in the early times of the Roman empire, Vitoria finds himself in a legal conundrum. He has already established that the Spanish empire does not have dominion in the New World, thus making it impossible to apply Spanish law to the situation of the New World. Therefore, Vitoria turns his attention to *ius gentium* in order to establish a legal framework by which he can evaluate both the presence of Spain and the existence of the natives in the New World.

It is important to note that prior to Vitoria there was "no coherent synthesis" of *ius gentium* to which Vitoria could appeal.[33] It is unsurprising to find fluidity in Vitoria's development and use of *ius gentium*, especially when one considers the fluidity and interchangeability of natural law and *ius gentium*.[34] This fluidity is especially evident when Vitoria states that *ius gentium* is both natural law and is derived from natural law. On the one hand, Vitoria equates *ius gentium* with natural law, thus making the former universally applicable to all humanity. On the other hand, Vitoria argues that *ius gentium*, similar to positive law, is derived from natural law. As developed by Vitoria, *ius gentium* carries with it not only an appeal to authority by virtue of its universality, but *ius gentium* also has the legal coercive power of positive law.

Again, what is important for Vitoria is to provide a legal framework by which he can evaluate the situation in the New World. Vitoria has therefore

---

31. Ibid., 37.

32. Nicholas, *Introduction*, 54–59.

33. Tierney, "Vitoria and Suarez," 4.

34. Stein, "Roman Law."

established a legal right that allows Spain to travel in the New World, but adds a restriction that is often overlooked: the right of Spain to travel in the New World is made void if the travelers are doing something evil in the foreign nations they are visiting.

Already, one must call into question Vitoria's confidence in Spain's right to travel in the New World. We should keep in mind that the occasion for the writing of *On the Indians* is the reported mistreatment of the natives by the Spaniards. In other words, cruel treatment of the natives by the Spanish is not questioned. What is questioned is the right of Spain to remain in the New World. Thus far, Vitoria has argued that Spain has no dominion, but is allowed to travel in the New World, provided that they do no harm to the natives. But, Vitoria has already granted that the Spaniards are acting cruelly toward the natives. Does Vitoria, then, believe that Spain has the right to be in the New World?

Brian Tierney has noted in his paper, "Vitoria and Suarez on *Ius Gentium*, Natural Law and Custom," that Vitoria presents arguments that he himself does not believe. "One has the impression that Vitoria himself was not convinced," writes Tierney, "by all the arguments that he put forward in favor of the Spaniards."[35] Of course, Vitoria's presentation of arguments of which he is unconvinced should come as no surprise, especially when one considers the fact that Vitoria makes use of the scholastic method, which often presents antagonists' arguments in the best possible light. Vitoria, therefore, is presenting possible claims that Spain may have to the New World, which may be unconvincing to Vitoria.

A second appeal to *ius gentium* is found in the second proposition of the third section.[36] According to Vitoria, the Spaniards have the right to trade with the barbarians, and to export any items, such as gold and silver, which the natives may have in abundance. This right, like others that he has presented, is based on *ius gentium*; but as he has previously done, here too Vitoria fails to reference specific Roman law. Vitoria seems to be developing *ius gentium* that would be applicable to both the Spanish and the natives. The barbarians, therefore, do not have the right to keep the Spaniards from conducting business transactions in the New World.

In addition to an appeal to *ius gentium*, Vitoria appeals to divine law to establish the right of the Spaniards to trade in the New World. The interesting aspect of this appeal is that, like *ius gentium*, it lacks any specific

35. Tierney, *Vitoria and Suarez*, 12.
36. Vitoria, *Obras*, 708.

reference to a Scriptural text or principle. Vitoria simply assumes that the readers will agree with him when he states that divine law allows the Spanish to trade.

Equally interesting is Vitoria's appeal to love. That Vitoria would argue that the barbarians are obliged to love the Spaniards is unsurprising, especially in view of the fact that he is a Catholic theologian and love is one of the Christian motivations for treating people with dignity. What is surprising is that Vitoria argues that natural law, rather than divine law, obliges the natives to love the Spaniards. Of course, Vitoria will maintain in his *Commentary* on Thomas Aquinas's *Summa* that both divine law and natural law have their origin in the eternal law of God. Nonetheless, his appeal to natural law for loving is another instance of Vitoria's innovativeness in that the natives, who are not Christians, and thereby not under the jurisdiction of the love command, are still obliged under the jurisdiction of natural law to love the Spaniards. Of course, as an empire that claims to be promoting the cause of Christ, the Spaniards are already obliged to love the natives.

As with the previous right, the Spanish right to trade in the New World has a condition: "it cannot be prohibited, if it is done without causing harm to the barbarians."[37] Again, the legal right to trade in the New World, including importing and exporting goods, is conditional on the humane treatment of the natives by the Spaniards, which is, of course, something that is difficult to establish. A theoretical approach to the rights of the Spanish empire to exist in the New World does not necessitate an acknowledgment of the just claim that Spain is making to their actual existence in the New World. In other words, Vitoria is envisioning possibilities for Spain to exist in the New World, but recognizes the inhumane treatment of the natives, which would call into question the rights that Spain is claiming. Therefore, from a theoretical perspective, Vitoria puts forward a framework that would justify the right of Spanish presence in the New World, but is marked by conditional phrases that also protect the rights of the natives to live without experiencing cruel treatment at the hands of the Spanish empire.

While there are many other occasions on which Vitoria appeals to *ius gentium*, the above uses exemplify the general idea that concerns Vitoria. This chapter's goal has been to consider how Vitoria develops *ius gentium* to defend the rights of the natives of the New World. First, we took note of Vitoria's argument that Spain lacks any right to exercise dominion in the

37. Ibid., 709.

New World. This argument is primarily based on the fact that the natives themselves have the right to exercise dominion, and, as such, their right to ownership cannot be denied. Second, in developing *ius gentium*, Vitoria establishes a legal framework that places both the Spanish and natives on equal ground by way of appealing to *ius gentium* to evaluate the duties and obligations of both parties. The legal structure has a coercive element because *ius gentium* is based on divine law and natural law, and is similar to positive law. Finally, when considering the rights of Spain to exist in the New World, Vitoria acknowledges these rights as long as certain conditions can be met, which is that the natives experience no harm at the hands of the Spanish. This final point calls into question whether Vitoria actually believed that Spain had a right to exist in the New World.

Faced with the Spanish legal framework that justified the cruel treatment of the natives in the New World, Vitoria develops another legal framework that supercedes that of the Spanish empire. It is a legal structure that recognizes the rights of both the Spanish and the natives. Likewise, it is a legal framework that is based on divine and natural law, as well as a newly developed notion of *ius gentium*, which is just as coercive—at least in the mind of Vitoria—as that of the Spanish empire. The force of the law that Vitoria proposed may be seen from the fact that Vitoria's *releccíon* was prevented from being published until well after his death.

3

Restraining Power in War

THIS CHAPTER WILL CONCENTRATE on Vitoria's *relección On the Right of War* or *On Just War* as it fits within the history of just war theory. This *relección* or lecture is a continuation of his previous *On the Indians*. The first *relección* was delivered on January 1539, and the second, six months later on June 18, 1539, as the Salamancan university term was coming to an end. We will see in this lecture what we have already perceived in the previous chapter: that Vitoria holds the Spanish emperor and empire accountable to law. To fully grasp the thrust of his argument I will briefly explore various other thinkers and their views of just war theory alongside Vitoria. By doing this I will situate Vitoria within his own time period but also demonstrate that he stands within a long history of just war thought. Consideration of these historical figures, then, is for the purposes of clarifying and grasping the full force of Vitoria's arguments. This is especially true as these figures shape the idea and practice of slavery. As he addresses his contemporary situation he develops arguments that go beyond the previous thinkers, though my focus is on those earlier thinkers who may have influenced Vitoria. I am indebted to the editors of *The Ethics of War* who have put together a one-volume history of just war theorists on which I draw occasionally in what follows, though I prefer to use the full texts when available.

Cicero (106–43 BCE)

I begin with Cicero, first, because he is the first to develop a "legal and normative framework for war,"[1] second, because of his influence in the Latin

1. Reichberg, *Ethics*, 51.

world, and, third, because of his prominent place in Vitoria's own writings. Cicero was born in 106 BCE to an influential family in Arpinum. No one in his family had ever held public office, so his rise to become the "chief magistra[te] in republican Rome"[2] was particularly unusual. In fact, his rise to office was the result of his having exposed the Catiline Conspiracy, which urged various aristocrats to rise up against the Republic, by reading letters of Catiline's plan to the Senate. Knowing the conspirators' plans, Cicero ambushed the conspirators in the countryside and had them executed in December 63 BCE. This event both led to Cicero's rise to prominence and became the reason for his exile in 58 BCE.

Cicero was quite familiar with such civil unrest. From the time that he began to study law with Quintus Mucius Scaevola in c. 89 there was civil unrest (BCE 88–82). Later in life he would encounter similar bloody events, including the civil war that began BCE 49, the murder of Pompey, the suicide of Cato, and the assassination of Caesar. It is after Caesar became the sole dictator of Rome that Cicero wrote *de officiis* (*On Duty*), the primary text in which he explicates his views on war.

There are three particular elements that I wish to discuss about Cicero's *On Duty*: first, that war must have a goal in order for it to be legitimate, and this goal is peace; second, that entering into war brings with it particular legal requirements of the warring parties; and third, that when taking up arms against another, war demands that one recognize the commonality one has with the other party.

According to Cicero, war ought always to be conducted with a goal in mind, this goal being peace. He writes, "Wars, then, ought to be undertaken for this purpose, that we may live in peace, without injustice."[3] Here Cicero notably connects the goal of war and the means to that goal. The goal should not be attained through means that though possible are questionable, i.e., unjust. Cicero insists that peace should "have nothing to do with treachery."[4] The achievement of peace through treachery results in circumstances that are unwelcome—such as Caesar's dictatorial rule in Rome that replaced the previously existent Republic.[5] To prevent that from happening, Cicero places limitations on sovereign power, for example that, "While a ruler may have the ability to declare war, he must declare war with

2. Cicero, *Commonwealth*, vii.

3. Cicero, *Duties*, bk. 1, sect. 35.

4. Ibid.

5. Ibid.

a clear purpose in mind, which is peace."[6] Even when a ruler is seeking to make a name for himself or herself, the clearly defined goal of peace must be ever present. Nonetheless, war cannot be conducted at whim, but must follow specific stages.

In addition to having peace as its goal, Cicero insists war must also be just, meaning that it must measure up to a particular set of standards. First, war must follow "a fair code [that] has been drawn up, in full accordance with religious scruple, in the fetial laws of the Roman people."[7] (The fetial was a type of priest who counseled the roman senate in matters of war.) The initial step is the *res repetuntur*, which is the declaration that a wrong be made right. If the offender has not responded within the thirty to thirty-three day period, then the fetial—*pater patratus*—declares the *bellum denuntiatur*, which is a "declaration to heaven that satisfaction had been denied, together with threat of war."[8] Afterwards the senate deliberates the issue at hand and then makes its recommendation to the Roman people of going to war, steps known as *senatus censet*. Once the deliberations are completed, there is an official ordering of war, termed *populous iubet*. The final step is the *bellum indicitur*, which is the throwing of a spear into the enemy's land as the official declaration of war. Cicero brings up the fetial not because of its religious aspect but rather to emphasize the legal aspects of going to war. In other words, while the ruler may have power, even he is required to comply with the demands of law. Cicero writes, "no war is just unless it is waged after a formal demand for restoration, or unless it has been formally announced and declared beforehand."[9] If war is conducted without the legal demands being met, then the war is unjust.

Cicero writes, "When, then, we are fighting for empire and seeking glory through warfare, those grounds that I mentioned a little above [peace] as just grounds for war should be wholly present." Cicero emphasizes being committed to the standards and guidelines he has stated for these have authority even when one is "seeking glory through warfare." Cicero argues that a government, even an empire, cannot go to war simply because it wants to. Governments are also held accountable to a standard of warfare.

This standard, or demand for justice, during warfare is based on the fact that war is conducted against fellow human beings. Cicero writes,

6. Ibid.

7. Ibid.

8. Oost, *Fetial*, 147–59, 148.

9. Cicero, *Duties*, bk. 1, sect. 36.

"The most widespread fellowship existing among men is that of all with all others."[10] This common bond to all others demands that one treat others in certain ways. He states, "one should not keep others from fresh water, should allow them to take fire from your fire, should give trustworthy counsel to someone who is seeking advice."[11] The first two rules reflect basic human survival needs—for water and for fire. The third, "trustworthy counsel," is hardly a survival need but it is a characteristic of being human that must be maintained in order to avoid injustice. "Injustice may be done," writes Cicero, "either through force or through deceit; and deceit seems to belong to the little fox, force to a lion. Both of them seem most alien to a human being."[12] For Cicero, being human entails a certain disposition toward others. In this case, honesty is a feature that should be present in all, even in times when keeping one's word would prove detrimental. "If any individuals have been constrained by circumstance to promise anything to an enemy, they must keep faith even in that," writes Cicero.[13] He even goes so far as to argue against a literal interpretation over and against one's intention. He writes, "For on the question of keeping faith, you must always think of what you meant, not of what you said."[14] It is always possible to find a way not to keep one's word, but Cicero puts in place a way of measuring whether one is being honest by asking about the intention of one's words. Cicero furthermore insists on refraining from being deceitful because the recipient of one's deceit would be none other than a fellow human being to whom is owed justice and not deceit.

Justice is due not only to one's equals but also to those of a lower social status. Cicero states, "Let us remember also that justice must be maintained even towards the lowliest."[15] The lowliest he has in mind here are the slaves, who nonetheless are human beings and must be treated accordingly. Rather than viewing slaves as slaves, Cicero suggests that one ought to view them as "employees" from whom one extracts work but to whom one also owes something, specifically justice. Here Cicero is challenging the legal notion of chattel, which is legal property one possesses. He insists that a slave not

---

10. Ibid., bk. 1, sect. 51.
11. Ibid., bk. 1, sect. 52.
12. Ibid., bk. 1, sect. 39.
13. Ibid.
14. Ibid., bk. 1, sect. 40.
15. Ibid.

be treated as chattel, but more like an employee because even the slave belongs to the "fellowship of the human race."[16]

Cicero juxtaposes property and human beings in order to recognize the value of the latter over the former. "Nothing is more the mark of a mean and petty spirit than to love riches," writes Cicero. He continues, "Nothing more honourable and more magnificent than to despise money if you are without it, but if you have it to devote it to liberality and beneficence."[17] "Love of riches" is set in contrast to "liberality" and "beneficence" because the former has oneself as the focus while the latter two focus on others by sharing one's wealth with others in need.

Cicero also recognizes that riches are often gained by taking advantage of others. He states, "For one man to take something from another and to increase his own advantage at the cost of another's disadvantage is more contrary to nature than death, than poverty, than pain and than anything else that may happen to his body or external possessions."[18] Taking advantage of others is going against one's very being, which implies that one is acting in a way that is less than human. Taking advantage of others also "destroys the common life and fellowship of men."[19] For Cicero it is important that human beings are social beings who relate to one another. Of course this "fellowship of men" does not imply that one simply puts others before oneself in terms of meeting the necessities for life, for this too would be against nature. Nature allows one to "secure for himself rather than for another anything connected with the necessities of life."[20] Nature allows the preservation of one's own life.

While nature has been the main focus for Cicero, he also introduces an idea that would later become prominent in Vitoria. Cicero writes, "The same thing is established not only in nature, that is in the law of nations, but also in the laws of individual peoples, through which the political community of individual cities is maintained." Here Cicero refers back to the previous notion that nature prohibits one from harming others in order to gain riches. There are three aspects to which he appeals to establish this notion, and one that is especially important to this project. The well-being of others is sustained by nature and the "laws of individual peoples," two

16. Ibid., bk. 1, sect. 21.
17. Ibid., bk. 1, sect. 68.
18. Ibid., bk. 1, sect. 21.
19. Ibid., bk. 1, sect. 21.
20. Ibid., bk. 1, sect. 22.

forces that while not necessarily equal to one another nonetheless both reinforce proper treatment of others. What is especially interesting is that Cicero equates nature with the law of nations so that by referring to the former one also refers to the latter. Yet Vitoria makes a distinction between the two. Following Cicero, he says that there are times that the law of nations is equal to nature. Mainly, however, Vitoria insists that the law of nations is above nature.

Finally, Cicero's idea of benevolence extends beyond one's community. He writes, "There are others again who say that account should be taken of other citizens, but deny it in the case of foreigners . . ."[21] Cicero appears to be concerned with those individuals who fail to see any duty to those who are outside of one's political society. This attitude excludes others simply because they are not participants in the local polis. However, Cicero widens political obligation to include those who are "foreigners" because to do otherwise would "tear apart the common fellowship of the human race." Furthermore, the failure to include the foreigners would "be thought more contrary to nature for one man to deprive another for the sake of his own advantage than to endure every disadvantage, whether it affects externals or the body or even the spirit itself—so long as it is free from injustice."[22] Cicero makes a distinctive connection between all people, a connection that transcends political, cultural, and social boundaries. Vitoria will pick up on many of these ideas and expand on them to address the situation in which he finds himself.

Augustine (354–430)

In Augustine we see the beginning of a theoretical approach to just war and an overarching concern for peace, which entails a tranquility of order that is dependent on political peace. While one may need to wage war in order to maintain this order, Augustine warns that war must be approached cautiously and should only be conducted in extreme circumstances when all other options have been exhausted.

Augustine's reflections on war must be considered in light of his understanding of what, in *The City of God*, he refers to as "the two cities." Here, Augustine introduces the notion that the heavenly city and the earthly city

21. Ibid., bk. 1, sect. 28.
22. Ibid.

are always in conflict with one another. This conflict is best understood in terms of love. This love can be of two kinds—*amor sui* and *amor dei*, which are also associated with two kinds of glories. He writes,

> Accordingly, two cities have been formed by two loves: the earthly by the love of self, even to the contempt of God; the heavenly by the love of God, even to the contempt of self. The former, in a word, glories in itself, the latter in the Lord. For the one seeks glory from men; but the greatest glory of the other is God, the witness of conscience.[23]

The two cities, interacting within our history, have two different purposes that are an intertwining of actions and motivation. Unfortunately, the earthly city is dominated by love of ruling and domination, coercion and vengeance, while the heavenly city is oriented by service and forgiveness. The goal of both cities is peace, but they seek to achieve it by two different means. The earthly city seeks calmness of the social order by resorting to domination and control. The second city, the heavenly city, seeks for God's reign.

Augustine is always mindful of the tension between the cities, and their desire for peace. On the one hand, Augustine is reluctant to espouse war, yet he recognizes its necessity at certain times. He writes, "Let them ask, then, whether it is quite fitting for good men to rejoice in extended empire." He continues, "For the iniquity of those with whom just wars are carried on favors the growth of a kingdom, which would certainly have been small if the peace and justice of neighbors had not by any wrong provoked the carrying on of war against them."[24] There are two issues that are especially important. First, Augustine contrasts a "good man" with one who rejoices over the expansion of empire, thereby demonstrating some hesitancy in the thought of rejoicing over the increase of the Roman empire. Second, Augustine suggests that growth of empire is the direct result of "iniquity" and "provocation." If justice and peace prevailed, then there would no necessity for war and no need for an enlargement of empire.

Augustine is well aware of human nature's desire to justify a questionable action. He writes, "Your wishes are bad, when you desire that one whom you hate or fear should be in such a condition that you can conquer him."[25] The conquest of an enemy is based on the condition that justifies

23. Augustine, *City*, 14.28 (Dyson, 633).
24. Ibid., bk. 6, chap. 15.
25. Ibid., bk, 4, chap. 15.

the conquest. Yet, the conqueror is lacking because he desires to find in the enemy, whom he "hates or fears," a justifiable reason for conquest. Just war in this case may be viewed as *cupiditas*, which is love turned in on oneself. Augustine speaks of the reaction that a wise man would have when he realizes the need for war—that of lament; but for one who is interested in expanding his empire, there is a sense of satisfaction that war is justifiable.[26] Augustine even refers to the desire to expand empire as sin. He writes, "This lust of sovereignty disturbs and consumes the human race with frightful ills."[27] There is, then, a relation between the desire for peace (concord) and the inner disposition of the individual (lust, desire to see evil in others), which creates a tension in Augustine. He recognizes that war is often necessary to secure peace, but the motive in achieving this goal is thwarted by the inner disposition of human beings. We want peace but often resort to questionable means to achieve it.

To overcome this tension between the desire for peace and the desire to see evil in others Augustine suggests that war should only be conducted to defend others as opposed to defending oneself. This emphasis is different from that of others such as Aquinas and Vitoria who argue that war may be conducted to defend oneself.[28] Augustine maintains there is something wrong with law when it allows one to act in an unjust way, such as killing a rapist before the actual rape has taken place. Law in this case would be unjust. This complex view of law is reminiscent of the view of peace Augustine portrays.

Returning to the dual cities: the nature of the earthly city is such that it will eventually cease to exist because it is not eternal. Augustine writes, "The earthly city will not last forever, for when it is condemned to final punishment, it will cease to be a city."[29] Only the heavenly city, the city of God, will endure. Notwithstanding its temporal nature, the earthly city has a certain quality that is considered to be good because, "It possesses its own good here and now, and it is made joyful through its association with the joy that may be derived from such things."[30] This position contrasts with his previous adherence to Manichean belief, which maintained that the material world was created by an evil power. In contrast, Augustine argues that

26. Ibid., bk. 19, chap. 7.

27. Ibid., bk. 3, chap. 14.

28. Reichberg, *Ethics*, 72–73.

29. Augustine, *City*, bk. 15, chap. 4.

30. Ibid.

even the earthly city has some good. Yet, the good does not necessitate the absence of "difficulties for its lovers." Caught in a conundrum of its own making, the earthly city "seeks to be the conqueror of peoples while being itself the captive of vices." Seeking peace, the earthly city finds itself in the midst of death. Augustine writes, "If indeed its pride is elevated because it conquers, then its victory causes death." In spite of these seemingly negative aspects of the earthly city, nonetheless Augustine makes the point that it desires and contains a certain kind of peace.

Indeed, Augustine recognizes some goodness in human beings and the institutions they develop and shape. He writes, "Anyone who pays any attention to human affairs and our common human nature recognizes as I do that just as there is no one who does not wish to be joyful, so there is no one who does not wish to have peace."[31] Even when war is waged it is done so with the goal of peace in mind. "Consequently," he writes, "the desired end of war is peace, for everyone seeks peace, even by waging war, but no one seeks war by making peace."[32] Realizing that the desire for peace occurs through the means of war is a complex notion of human existence. Yet, the goal—peace—is admirable and good. This is a lesson that one should learn when considering empires and colonialism.[33]

If Augustine is correct when he states that all desire peace, then empires such as that of the Spanish, English, Incas, Aztecs, and Americans have peace as their goal. The problem with such empires is the means by which they seek to reach the goal. If one critiques the fact that empires seek to expand their borders, one confronts the most central reality of empires, for this is what empires seek to do. Empires expand. A critique of empire, therefore, results in a critique of its very nature, which appears nonsensical. Yet the acknowledgement of the expansion of empires is by no means acquiescence to the cruelties that are carried out. This acknowledgment is simply a realistic view of what is part and parcel of empire. As such, it is necessary to work within the empire and hold it accountable to its own

31. Augustine, *City*, bk. 19, chap. 12.

32. Ibid.

33. It seems that one of the difficulties with works by Todorov, Williams, and Rivera-Pagán is that their view of empire and colonialism is one-dimensional, especially when they consider the Spanish empire of the sixteenth century. The prevailing conclusion is that Spain was mostly interested in the conquest and subjugation of the natives. Most things associated with Spain are considered as having a negative effect on the natives; the *encomienda* system, the *requerimiento*, and the desire to convert the natives to Christianity are all viewed with suspicion as means of controlling and subduing the natives.

goals and expectations as well as holding it accountable to outside sources that could be recognized and accepted, i.e., God, natural law, international law, etc.

My goal is to glean from historical figures such as Vitoria and develop a critique that recognizes the legitimacy of empires and the need to defend human rights. At the same time, one must recognize that empires and even our critical approaches are human, and as such are susceptible to errors and shortcomings.

Augustine recognized that peace is desired and sought after by all people but also that peace will never be fully achieved in this present world. He states, "Whoever hopes for so great a good as is promised to David in this world and on this earth shows all the understanding of a fool." He continues, "Does anyone really think that the promise of such a good was fulfilled in the peace that existed during the reign of Solomon?" Having dismissed the notion that peace may be fully established on earth he states, "Therefore, that place which is promised to be such a peaceful and secure dwelling is eternal, and is owed to the eternal ones in Jerusalem, the free mother."[34] While Augustine recognizes that peace is essentially eternal, he restrains himself from criticizing worldly peace. Instead, he makes a clear distinction between the two. The fact that peace cannot ultimately be attained while on earth does not call into question the legitimacy of its pursuit because the latter is necessary. But he would say that equally necessary is the use of coercive power to achieve peace.

War is necessary for the establishment of peace. However, war must be declared by a legitimate authority. "The natural order, which is suited to the peace of mortal things, requires that the authority and deliberation for undertaking war be under the control of a leader," states Augustine.[35] Only one who has been bestowed with the authority to declare war is able to do so. Another individual who seeks to go to war without the proper authority goes against the established order. According to Augustine, the right to declare war is aligned with the "natural order." Only a legitimate ruler or leader is able to declare war because authority "has been given to him from above." Augustine references Romans 13:1 to establish the idea that authority to declare war comes from God.[36] Here one finds the foundational idea that government and rulers come from God, which will become

---

34. Augustine, *City*, bk. 17, chap. 13.

35. Augustine, *Augustine*, 222–23.

36. Ibid.

the standard in the medieval ages and remain so even up to the cusp of the modern era in Francisco Vitoria.

This notion is one that scholars who adopt a postcolonial critique especially spurn because they tend to emphasize the unjust practices and oppression that governments participate in against various groups and individuals who are not participants of the wider body politic. The downside of such an approach is that it makes it virtually impossible to identify any positive characteristics of a government or leader. In general, what is perceived are the extreme injustices that these political bodies are involved in while disregarding any good they may produce. The result of such a perspective is the desire to see the political bodies overthrown so that the unjust practices may cease and/or be overcome by another political body. For Augustine, however, even those political entities that are cruel and oppressive are legitimate.

Viewing political bodies as legitimate does not necessitate the acceptance of unlimited political power. In fact, for Augustine, legitimate powers must be sure to use their strength to defend against threats. He writes, "As a rule just wars are defined as those which avenge injuries."[37] Just wars are punitive in that they are specifically conducted against injuries that have already taken place in reality and not merely against perceived threats. Once the injury has taken place then war is fully justified. However, if the injury has already been avenged, and the rightful parties have been punished, then war is not an option. Augustine's previous thought continues when he writes, "if some nation or state against whom one is waging war has neglected to punish a wrong committed by its citizen, or to return something that was wrongfully taken,"[38] in short, if the wrong is not avenged or made right, then the state has the right to take justice into its own hands.

To be sure, the right to take justice into one's own hands does not give one a license to act without restraint. In *The City of God* Augustine refers to the recent devastation he has witnessed when he states, "All the devastation, the butchery, the plundering, the conflagrations, and all the anguish which accompanied the recent disaster at Rome were in accordance with the general practice of warfare,"[39] in order to emphasize the merciful treatment of those who gathered at the basilicas, because of which the "barbarians took on such an aspect of gentleness."[40] The emphasis here should be on those

---

37. Swift, *Early Fathers*, 135.

38. Ibid..

39. Augustine, *City*, bk. 1, chap. 7.

40. Ibid.

who gathered at the basilicas as non-combatants as opposed to individuals who were directly involved in the battle, i.e., soldiers. Just war, therefore, takes heed of those who are non-combatants in order to spare their lives. Not surprisingly he maintains that this merciful act of the barbarians is the result of God's power rather than the barbarians' own doing. What is important for him is that even the barbarians showed restraint in time of war. In a letter to Boniface, Augustine is especially clear on the mercy that ought to be shown in times of war. He states, "Let necessity slay the warring foe, not your will. As violence is returned to one who rebels and resists, so should mercy be to one who has been conquered or captured, especially when there is no fear of a disturbance of peace."[41] War, then, is not simply about invasion, expansion, and victory. For Augustine, war is much more complex and demands a realistic view of the political circumstances that are present.

In sum, for Augustine all acts done by a political body are done for some good in that they are seeking some good. From a political perspective all peace is tranquility of order, and, as such, war can be waged for the sake of restoring this order. The City of God and the city of man are in constant conflict with one another, which provides the theological context for entertaining justifiable warfare. This context limits the lethal force that one is allowed to use because war should only be undertaken in extreme circumstances.

While Augustine may espouse the violence of war he has a profound bias against war. Yet, he recognizes the necessity of war for the greater good, which is peace. Therefore, war must always be defensive and non-aggressive. This demands thoughtfulness about the ends and means of war. Concerning the end of war there must be justifiable engagement, or rather, a just cause must be present, one that seeks peace rather than vengeance or annihilation. War must be the last resort and must be declared by a legitimate authority.

Finally, Augustine is concerned with the moral conduct of war. Non-combatants are to be spared from the violence of war. There must be discrimination during acts of violence. Those who are not soldiers ought to be spared and not slaughtered. Also, there must be proportionality in war. The end, which is peace, must outweigh the destruction that is brought about through war.

41 Augustine, *Augustine*, 220.

All in all, Augustine recognizes that Christians are citizens and part of a political body. As such, they are confronted with the problem of participating in a legitimate war. His conception of a just war takes into account the actual and real political realities of social existence in this world. When we turn our attention to Francisco Vitoria we will notice he expresses some of the same concerns as Augustine. But before we turn to Vitoria, we first look briefly at Gratian's *Decretum*.

Gratian (Twelfth Century)

Gratian and his texts are important not only because Francisco Vitoria frequently refers to them, but also because of their centrality to the study of law, specifically ecclesial law. The study of law came to prominence with the discovery of the Justinian text in 1080 CE, which would come to be known as the *Corpus Iuris Civilis*. The Justinian *Code* was compiled by 534 CE, and consisted of the *Code*, the *Digest*, and the *Institutes*. While the Roman law, as compiled by Justinian, was lost as a complete text after the sixth century, fragments survived within the Frankish and Germanic legal systems.[42] It was not until the eleventh century that the Roman law once again came to prominence.

In 1087 CE, Irnerius began to teach in Bologna, northern Italy. Shortly after the Justinian *Code* was rediscovered Irnerius taught from the *Code* and founded the school of glossators. This school at Bologna became the most sought after place at which to study law.[43] Whereas ecclesial law had previously been taught at Bologna, the study of Roman law soon predominated and Irnerius's influence soon extended beyond the field of civil law. In addition to Irnerius, Gratian was also at Bologna.

There is some question as to Gratian's actual dates, but there is some certainty that he was deceased by 1160 CE.[44] His influence and works made an impact during his life and beyond. The *Decretum* is a body of ecclesial laws that Gratian put together and analyzed in order to reach some agreement concerning particular subjects. It is composed of biblical texts, church council reports, sermons, works from the early church fathers, papal decrees, and so forth. Gratian may not have worked with the original

42. Berman, *Law and Revolution*, 122.

43. Gratian et al., *Treatise on Laws*, xi.

44. Ibid., x.

texts of all of these, but he had access to them through other texts on which he worked. What is important is how Gratian "selected, organized, and analyzed" these texts.[45]

Of the many subjects that Gratian covers we will look at the issue of war. This is not always a straightforward matter, since he often broached the topic only indirectly, and was concerned mostly with ecclesial law and cases of heresy and lapsed bishops, as found in causa 23. Causa 23 considers the use of violence and coercion from a religious point of view, specifically that of Christianity. Here, Gratian considers this question by entertaining Augustine's position and providing an elucidation of his own view. While causa 23 has eight questions that consider war and coercion, I will focus only on those issues that are particularly relevant to this book and argument.

The central issue that Gratian raises in question two of causa 23 has to do with defining what constitutes a just war. He has already considered whether Christians are able to participate in warfare, especially in light of the gospel teachings. While he answers in the affirmative, Gratian also cautions against rushing into war, reminding the reader to consider various questions, among them being whether or not the war is just.

For Gratian, a "war is just which is waged by an edict in order to regain what has been stolen or to repel the attack of enemies."[46] There are two elements here that are especially important for our purposes. First, the act of war demands a legal and political pronouncement. Implied is that the pronouncement must come from a figure who has the authority to issue such an edict. Gratian writes, "A judge is called such because he pronounces justice to the people, or because he adjudicates justly."[47] This is similar to what we have in Augustine who argues that war cannot proceed without there first being a declaration of war.

The second element that is particularly important for our purposes is that war is to be conducted in reaction to either a theft or an attack. In the former case, one is seeking to recover what was stolen. In the latter, war is defensive. In any case, war is never initiated without due cause; it is always defensive. Again, this is similar to what we considered in Augustine who argued that war must be defensive. Gratian also argues that war should be conducted for the purposes of protection. He writes, "The

45. Ibid., xiii.
46. Reichberg, *Ethics*, 109.
47. Ibid., 113.

courage that protects one's country form barbarians in war, or defends the weak in peace, or associates against brigands, is full of justice."[48] War, in this instance, is for the protection of the innocent—often the ones who lack the ability to protect themselves—against those who wish to destroy them. This weakness allows those with power (in this case, the judge,) to declare war as a way of protecting them.

The notion of protecting others is in contrast to those who simply want to seek vengeance. Gratian makes this distinction when he writes, "From all this we gather that vengeance is to be inflicted not out of passion for vengeance itself . . . but out of zeal of justice; not in order that hatred be vented, but that evil deeds be corrected."[49] He clearly sets out the purposes of war, which are justice and correction. Explicitly prohibited here is the unbridled passion of vengeance that often accompanies the desire to make right that which was wronged. While there is a notion of retribution and retaliation here, these must be entered into cautiously, meaning that one must be concerned with the inner disposition of the one who has declared war. Vengeance must be based on justice rather than hatred of the one who has committed the wrong act. Here, Gratian is interested in both the victim and the attacker. The victim, though justified in seeking vengeance, must be attentive to his inner disposition. Likewise, the goal of punishing the criminal is not a reprisal as such, but an act of correction.

With the notion that war is for the purpose of correction rather than vengeance, we are now able to return to Canon 3 of Question II in order to consider Gratian's use of Augustine in defining just war. As mentioned previously, Gratian follows Augustine's definition of just war by quoting from the latter's work on the book of Numbers. As understood by Gratian, the sons of Israel waged a just war against the Amorites. In itself this is not very interesting. But what is interesting is the reason that the war is considered just. The sons of Israel waged a just war, "For they were denied innocent passage, which ought to have been granted according to the most equitable law governing human society."[50] Reacting to the Amorites' refusal to allow Israel to travel freely through its borders, the Israelites take up arms. Not only do they go to war, they justify the act of war by the Amorites' refusal to let them travel through their land. Furthermore, as understood by both Augustine and Gratian, the right to travel through the land of the Amorites is

48. Ibid., 114.

49. Ibid., 116.

50. Ibid., 113.

a right due to the Israelites "according to the most equitable law governing human society."

Of interest is that both Augustine and Gratian fail to mention where the "equitable law" can be found and known. Augustine, of course, may have in mind that law which all people know and to which they have access. Similarly, Gratian may also have in mind natural law, which can be known through reason. However, it is likely that here Gratian has in mind Roman law as found within Justinian's *Institutes*.

According to Justinian's *Institutes* all people are to have access to the sea-shores because they "are naturally everybody's."[51] The right to the sea-shores is based on the law of nations, or as Justinian prefers, the law of all people. One finds in the *Institutes*,

> The law of all peoples allows public use of river banks, as of the rivers themselves; everybody is free to navigate rivers, and they can moor their boats to the banks, run ropes from trees growing there, and unload cargo.

A difference between Gratian's reading of the "equitable law" and the "law of peoples" is that the former deals with individuals who are traveling through the land, while the latter is primarily concerned with various vessels being fastened to the shore. If Gratian has in mind Roman law to justify his position that Israel was in the right to go against the Amorites in war, then he is adopting a very loose interpretation of Roman law. However, there is no clear indication that he even has Roman law in mind.

I have mentioned Roman law in this instance, although it appears that Gratian does not specifically refer to it, because Francisco Vitoria will do what Gratian does not. We have already seen that Vitoria argues that Spain has the right to land in the New World, to travel throughout the land, and to trade with the natives. Vitoria argues that this right remains intact as long as the Spaniards do not harm the natives. This position is similar to Roman law, which states that those who have come on-shore "must keep away from houses, monuments, and buildings."[52] While they may have the right to moor, they lack the right to the possessions of the inhabitants. Vitoria adopts a similar line of thought.

Gratian is important to our purposes because he serves as a bridge between Roman law and canon law, organizing a variety of religious texts

51. Justinian, *Institutes*, 55.
52. Ibid.

and commentaries to address questions in a systematic and logical manner.[53] In short, Gratian adopts a scholastic approach to the study of law. This, then, opens the path for individuals such as Vitoria to consider practical problems and apply the body of the law as a means of analysis and the search for justice.

Thomas Aquinas (1225–1274)

We turn next to Thomas Aquinas's three-part understanding of just war. Besides considering Aquinas because of his scholastic approach of bringing together previous sources, it is also important to consider him because of the great influence he had in the sixteenth century, especially in the writings of Cajetan, and our primary figure, Francisco Vitoria.

Aquinas's contribution to just war theory is the logical approach that later individuals such as Bartolus, Cajetan, and Vitoria adopted. He tackles it in the *Secundae secundae* of the *Summa Theologica*, which is where he takes up the issue of the theological virtues—faith, hope, and charity. It is within the discussion of the third virtue that Thomas raises the question of war.

As understood by Aquinas, there are three conditions for a just war. First, an individual who goes to war must have the authority to call for and enact a war. A private individual lacks this authority. Aquinas states, "For it is not the business of a private individual to declare war, because he can pursue his right before the judgment of his superior."[54] Rather than taking matters into his own hands, the private individual is able to appeal to a higher authority for justice. Likewise, this individual lacks the ability to call others together in his defense. "Moreover it is not the business of a private person to summon together the people, which has to be done in wartime," writes Aquinas.[55] Only a person who has the authority as ruler is able to call people together for the sake of war.

In addition to having this authority, the ruler has the responsibility to care for the society over which he rules. Aquinas writes, "And as the care of the common weal is committed to those who are in authority, it is their business to watch over the common weal of the city, kingdom or province

---

53. Berman, *Law and Revolution*, 146.

54. Aquinas, *Summa*, II–II Q. 40, Art. 1.

55. Ibid.

subject to them."[56] The idea of care over the "common weal" is based on the notion that the ruler has received this responsibility from God, as we read in Rom 13:4. The biblical text refers to the ruler as "God's minister." Actually, a careful consideration of the biblical text reveals that the text refers to the sword that the authority figure has and which is used to "punish malefactors."[57]

This reference is rather brief and without explication in Aquinas, whereas Cajetan develops it much more fully when he comments on the *Summa*. Likewise, it is a notion from which Vitoria wishes to distance himself when writing about the natives in the New World. Aquinas simply provides a brief reference and then moves on to the second condition for a just war.

In addition to having the proper authority to conduct a just war, Aquinas argues that a just war is in response to an attack of some kind. A just war requires, "that those who are attacked, should be attacked because they deserve it on account of some fault."[58] For Aquinas, war is not preemptive. Instead, it is always in response to a wrong that has been done. Of course, this is the same position argued by Augustine. Aquinas adds nothing to Augustine's position, whereas Vitoria broadens the condition by arguing for the possibility of a war being just from both sides of the war.

The third condition mentioned by Aquinas is that a just war must have as its purpose a right intention. He writes, "it is necessary that those waging war should have a rightful intention, so that they intend the advancement of good, or the avoidance of evil."[59] The goal of war is not the destruction of one's enemies, but rather peace. As Aquinas argues in his third reply, "Those who wage war justly aim at peace, and so they are not opposed to peace, except to the evil peace."[60]

In summary: concerning war Aquinas notes, first, the need, or duty, to defend the common good. Implied in this duty is the notion that inactivity is just as sinful as the unjust action of one who is attacking. Second, unlike others prior to him, Aquinas insists that all three criteria must be met: the proper authority must declare war, there must be a just cause, and the intention must be right.

56. Ibid.
57. Ibid.; Rom 13:4.
58. Ibid.
59. Ibid.
60. Ibid.

True to the scholastic method of considering a variety of perspectives and organizing them into a whole, Aquinas reiterates some of the conclusions previous thinkers reached. For example, similar to Cicero and Augustine, he recognizes the needs for proper authorities to enact war and the need to have peace as the ultimate goal. Nonetheless, Aquinas adds little to the general understanding of just war; he does not add any creative insights. Creativity will come with the next three figures that we will be considering.

Bartolus of Saxoferrato (1313–1357)

While this consideration of Bartolus of Saxoferrato will be brief it is nonetheless important. This section will focus primarily on his notion of citizen rights and the law of postliminy. This law has to do with the rights of those individuals who have been captured during the time of war, but are later returned to their former condition. To fully explicate what is meant by postliminy, Bartolus, as a true scholastic, takes the initial step of clarifying terms.

Bartolus distinguishes the meaning of "enemy" by considering the sense in which the individual is considered an enemy and who considers the individual an enemy. First, there is the individual who is an enemy of the city but not of the Roman people. Bartolus writes, "it would seem that any city would have its enemies, such as those against whom a city declares public war."[61] Such enemies are specific to the locale of the city; they would not, for example, automatically be enemies of the Roman people too. As such, the "laws of captivity and postliminy" do not apply.

This kind of confrontation would not be considered a real "war" because it is taking place within the city. War, for Bartolus, is reserved for the confrontation that takes place against the "Roman People" in a very public setting. Likewise, the term "enemy" is not applied to those who are attacking the city. He writes, "'Enemies' are those upon whom the Roman People has publicly declared war, or those who have themselves declared war upon the Roman People; the rest are called brigands or robbers."[62] The category "enemies," therefore, is reserved for those who are not associated with the Roman People; they are the foreigners.

61. Reichberg, *Ethics*, 205.
62. Ibid.

The distinction between "enemy" and "brigand" and "robber" is important for Bartolus because only an enemy is able to make its captives into slaves. Those captured by robbers and brigands are simply captured by them, but do not therefore belong to them. The difference between the two confrontations is that one is public and the second is private. In the latter case, while it could be termed a "war" it is not a "public war" against the "Roman People."

Bartolus's distinction between "public war" and a feudal "war" depends on the identity of the one who is attacking. If the attacker is from one's city/state, then the attack would be a "feudal" war. On the other hand, an attack against the People of Rome would be an act of war. To be sure, it is possible for someone with the proper jurisdiction within the city/state to declare war against those who are attacking. Such an act of warfare would be a just war. He writes, "[A]nyone having jurisdiction can declare a lawful war in the exercise of his jurisdiction."[63] The issue here is not whether one has jurisdiction (as we have seen with Augustine and Gratian). Bartolus is more interested in the identity of the individual with whom one is going to war.

The identity of one's attacker is important because it is a distinction of belonging. For Bartolus, there are two types of people, which is a notion that goes against the gloss he is referring to and against convention. "You should know that there are in principle two sorts of peoples, first, the Roman People; second, foreign peoples, as is proven above," writes Bartolus. The criteria for belonging to the Roman People is broad and includes not only those who reside within the empire's borders, but also those individuals who do not obey the emperor because they have been granted this liberty from the emperor. However, this is a privilege that, "in a certain way they hold . . . precariously, and [the emperor] could revoke this privilege whenever he wishes, since it is permissible for him to alter his will."[64] The common characteristic of the Roman People is that they are in some way, either explicitly or implicitly, accountable to the emperor. On the other hand, if there is no accountability, then that individual would be considered a foreigner.

Bartolus writes, "In the second place I said that the other peoples are foreign. Those are properly foreign peoples who do not acknowledge that

63. Ibid., 207.
64. Ibid., 206.

the Roman emperor is the universal ruler."[65] Groups that are included under this description are the Greeks, Tartars, and the Turks. Common to these groups is their allegiance to someone other than the Roman emperor. For instance, the Greeks argue that the emperor of Constantinople is the ruler over the entire world. The Tartars would make a parallel claim to the Greeks by stating that the Khan is the ruler of the world.

The importance of ascertaining whether the attacked is a foreigner or of the Roman People has to do with how one views what things and what people have been taken in the war. In the case of "feudal" wars, "those who are captured do not belong to the captors, and the captives do not become slaves."[66] Bartolus recognizes that these captors could become slaves, but whether this happens depends on legal matters that took place prior to the conflict. He writes, "and the slaves do not become slaves, unless some decree or sentence intervenes over this beforehand."[67] It appears, then, that prior to the conflict there had to be a conscious decision to take the captors as slaves. On this, Bartolus helpfully reports on how the decree or sentence would take shape. The making of captors into slaves has to be "promulgated . . . by the general or the commander or the king who declared the war."[68] Again, this conflict is between cities that are under a single ruler such as the emperor. As citizens of the emperor's empire those who have been captured have certain rights, which include protection from being enslaved. Likewise, those who have been captured could be enslaved, but a previous promulgation of law or a decree would have had to take place prior to the conflict. If no such decree is declared, then the captive cannot be enslaved because they are under the oversight of the ruler, i.e., the emperor.

In the case of war with foreign people, captives become slaves of those who captured them, and the possessions captured also belong to the victors.[69] Similarly, concerning the people captured, he writes, "the captives become slaves."[70] The basis for this assertion is the law of captivity and postliminy. According to the *Digest* 49, 15, 21, it is unnecessary for an individual who has been captured, sold, and then "manumitted" to request a restoration of their citizenship rights because in the case of a conflict between

65. Ibid., 207.
66. Ibid., 208.
67. Ibid.
68. Ibid.
69. Ibid.
70. Ibid.

cities citizenship is never lost.[71] However, when war is with enemies that seek to overthrow the empire, then the law of postliminy takes effect.

Ulpian gives us an example of postliminy in the *Digest*. His example is of a woman who is freeborn but has been captured by an enemy. An individual ransoms her from the enemy in order to have children. Later he "manumits a son born to her, along with the mother, under the designation of his natural son."[72] Ulpian makes the case that with postliminy she has returned, "free and freeborn," and "has produced a freeborn son."[73] However, if the mother is recovered by the soldiers, and the "father did not pay a ransom for the mother," then she is under no obligation in terms of servitude to the father. Nonetheless, a bond of matrimony remains in effect. Ulpian states, "she is forthwith declared to have returned with *postliminium*, not with a master but with a husband."[74] While the woman is restored to her previous state, her current state of marriage is not dissolved but rather is integrated into her previous position. What is important is the citizenship status of the woman, which is never called into question. Instead, the rights of the citizen are acknowledged and implemented in the status of the woman.

At issue in the above consideration is the status of those who have been captured. The capture of foreigners results in their slavery, and their possessions are bequeathed to the captors. However, if those captured are not foreigners, and are under an authority that is common to both the captors and the captured, then slavery is annulled because citizenship is never called into question.

Returning to Bartolus, the issue of war must be considered while taking into account the status of the one who has been captured. In the case of wars between cities the rights of citizenship is never called into question because even if an individual is taken captive, that same individual would still retain the rights of citizen, which would keep the individual from becoming a slave. Of course, Bartolus acknowledges that this could change if the prince were to state that those taken captive were to become slaves. In this instance the promulgation of law is necessary. In the case of war against enemies of the empire, captives lose the rights of citizens because they are no longer part of the empire, albeit not by choice. However, if the

71. Watson, *Digest*, 49, 15, 21.

72. Ibid., 15, 21.

73. Ibid.

74. Ibid.

captives return to the empire, then the full rights of citizenship are granted. Again, the issue of the status of the captured is especially important because it determines whether or not those captured are considered slaves or, in contemporary terms, prisoners of war.

For our purposes, the discussion of citizenship is especially relevant when we consider Francisco Vitoria's notion of just war. Does he consider the natives of the New World to be citizens of the Spanish empire? If so, then the natives would have particular rights that would not be granted to slaves. Further, is the concept of postliminy found in his writings? These two ideas, the rights of citizenship and postliminy, are seldom if ever considered when reading the texts of Vitoria. But before turning our attention to Francisco Vitoria, we must consider the work of Thomas de Vio (referred to as Cajetan from here on in) because of his influence on neo-scholasticism through his commentary on Aquinas's *Summa*. Also, Cajetan is an important figure to consider because Vitoria will try to distance himself from Cajetan's position when considering just war.

Thomas de Vio (Cajetan) (1469–1534)

Cajetan began his career at the University of Padua as a professor of metaphysics. He spent much time studying humanism. These studies catapulted him to a position that pitted him against Pico della Mirandola in a public debate at Ferrara in 1494, of which he was perceived so overwhelmingly to be the victor that his students carried him out on their shoulders after the debate. This debate, along with his great learning, propelled his career as a learned theologian and scholar. Following his appointment as Cardinal and Archbishop of Palermo, Cajetan was appointed as a legate to Germany. It was at the Diet of Augsburg in 1518 that Martin Luther appeared before Cajetan.[75] A year later Cajetan assisted in putting together the bull of excommunication of Luther. Among the many works that he produced, Cajetan's most impressive is his commentary on Aquinas's *Summa Theologica*, which is the focus of this section on Cajetan.

The most creative aspect of Cajetan's works is the distinction he makes between defensive and offensive wars. Prior to Cajetan, just wars were limited to defensive wars. Cajetan, breaking away from previous thinkers of just war, argues that a just war can be either offensive or defensive. In

---

75. Oberman, *Luther*, 23.

reference to defensive war, Cajetan is similar to his predecessors in arguing that individuals have a "natural right" to defend themselves against any attacks.[76] Of course, he recognizes the vast difference between an individual's right to defend oneself and the right of a prince. The difference between the two is more than the right to declare war. Private defense and public defense is differentiated by the extent of force that is available. Cajetan writes, "For a private person has but the right to repel force by force with the moderation of blameless defense."[77] He continues his elaboration by stating, "But it is beyond 'the moderation of blameless defense' for a private person to seek revenge for himself or others, just as it is not permitted for a private person to kill the killer of his own father."[78] The private person is limited to the force that is used in the attack; one can counter with only as much force as was used in the original attack. Also, one does not have the right to use force that would result in the punishment of the attacker. This right belongs to another.

For Cajetan, the state, or commonwealth, has the right "to exact revenge for injuries to itself or its members—not only against its subjects, but also against foreigners."[79] Here he has in mind more than simply defending oneself, specifically the right to exert punishment on those who attacked the commonwealth. The basis for his view is, "because punitive justice is the sole right of the commonwealth."[80] For a commonwealth to lack the ability to exert punitive justice would make it, "imperfect and defective," because "tyrants and rapacious villains, murderers, robbers, and any other people causing injury to the citizens of a foreign commonwealth would remain naturally unpunished, and natural reason would come to fail in these necessary matters."[81] In addition to the imperfection of a commonwealth, the inability to punish is an assault on "natural reason, which is of a greater ambit providentially than the natural instinct of animals, would be deficient by not providing the commonwealth with the power of revenge."[82] For Cajetan, the rational abilities and exercise would be called into question if the commonwealth were prohibited from meting out vindictive justice. It

76. Reichberg, *Ethics*, 242.

77. Ibid.

78. ibid.

79. Ibid.

80. Ibid.

81. Ibid.

82. Ibid., 243.

would be an act of violence against reason, which, in turn, would appear as an attack on the very nature of God.

By now, it is evident that Cajetan's analysis of just war is replete with legal language such as justice, punishment, and revenge. These references are especially important in light of his analysis set within the confines of a court proceeding.[83] Commenting on the right to go to war he concludes, "if justice is hoped for before war is declared, justice should be sought from his superior, because the plaintiff follows the court of the respondent." For Cajetan, the right to go to war is based not only on the privileges of the prince, but relies on the legality of such action. The right is inherent to the prince, but is also based on the demands of law. Justice demands punishment of wrongdoing. This is so true that in the case of two warring princes the one in the wrong becomes inferior to the prince who has been offended. Cajetan writes, "For the one passively disposed is confronting a just war because he refuses to offer satisfaction."[84] The act of wrongdoing makes one inferior and subject to vindictive punishment by the other who has been offended or is responding to someone who has been offended. Recall that only a proper authority figure has the right to distribute vindictive punishment.

While an individual has the right to defend herself against attacks by another, only a proper authoritative figure is able to declare war against an attacker. Especially important is the distinction that Cajetan makes concerning individuals who have the right to declare war. There is no question as to the limitation that is placed on the individual who has been attacked by an assailant; he is allowed to defend himself, but can only do so to the point of resisting the assailant. Resisting the assailant does not entail an offensive attack on the assailant. This is reserved for the agent who has the authority and power to organize and implement an offensive attack that serves as the means to vindictive justice. The distinction between having the right to defend oneself, which all possess, and the right to organize an offensive war, which only an authoritative figure possesses, must be kept in mind.

For Cajetan, it is possible for an individual to have limited authority in his exercise of vindictive authority. He writes, "There are many, however, who may use the sword by commission against natives."[85] Here, the ones he identifies as natives are not identical to the natives found in the New World.

83. Ibid., 241.
84. Ibid., 241, 243.
85. Ibid., 245.

Rather, natives are the individuals who live in and are part of the *civitas* or town. The authority of those who "use the sword by commission" are limited by the borders of their authority. They "are not allowed to declare war against foreigners."[86] This authority is reserved for "governors, cities, and many rulers who in their territories judge in capital cases." The reason for their limited authority is "this authority is easier for perfect princes to concede than the authority against foreigners."[87] Authority, then, is limited to those over whom the prince has direct oversight. Those who "use the sword by commission" can only exercise this authority over those who are directly under his supervision as he has no authority over those outside his borders because they are foreigners.

This issue will be especially important for Vitoria because it has to do with who has the authority to declare war. If the ruthless attack against the inhabitants of the New World is sanctioned by the emperor, then it is conducted on legal grounds. Of course, this has little impact on the justness of the war because it must follow a particular set of standards for it to be considered a just war. Similarly, for Vitoria, the issue is not simply whether the emperor has the right to declare a just war. Vitoria also raises the issue of the civic status of the inhabitants. Are they included in the Spanish empire? If so, then those individuals in Spain who have the authority to "use the sword by commission," as stated by Cajetan, would be justified in declaring a just war, but only if the demands of a just war were met. As Cajetan puts it, "If a just cause or proper authority is lacking in war, it is not a war at all, but an invasion, murder, and rapine."[88] Related to authority is the issue of whether the inhabitants of the New World are foreigners or citizens of the Spanish empire. If the inhabitants are not identified with the empire and are foreigners, then the war can only be declared by the perfect prince i.e., the emperor. This will be discussed even more when focus on Vitoria.

Before taking our leave of Cajetan we ought to spend some time considering the limitations he puts on war. In scholastic fashion, Cajetan raises an issue and then considers various approaches to the posed problem. He asks succinctly, "whether, after the onset of war, he who has a just war is required to desist from the war, if the iniquitous enemy offers satisfaction."[89] At issue here is the responsibility that the prince has toward those whom he

86. Ibid.
87. Ibid.
88. Ibid., 246.
89. Ibid., 247.

has attacked in a just war. Is the prince given free reign in carrying out a just war, even if the war is for the purposes of vindictive punishment? Similar questions have been posed throughout the history of just war theory, are picked up by Cajetan, and later by Francisco Vitoria.

According to Cajetan, it is necessary to distinguish three stages of war: "the beginning, the middle, and the near end."[90] If the war has yet to begin, but the troops are assembled to attack each other, and the "iniquitous enemy" offers to make satisfaction for the wrong that has taken place, then the prince is obligated "to accept the satisfaction and call off the war."[91] This limitation is placed because "warring does not depend on will but on necessity." In the present case where the enemy has offered satisfaction, "the necessity for war has ended."[92] Satisfaction of this kind is complete in that it is for "injuries and properties, but also concerning expenses and damages."[93]

Once a war has begun the above limitations are no longer valid because "he who has a just war is not required to end the war merely because the enemy now offers satisfaction."[94] To justify his position Cajetan returns to the use of court metaphors. Commenting on the reason for not needing to call a halt to war, he writes, "The reason for this is that the prosecutor of the just war functions as a judge of criminal proceedings."[95] This role as a judge is a result of the "just" nature of the war, which, in turn, allows the prince to engage in vindictive justice."[96] Worthy of note is Cajetan's reasoning for the prince's role as judge. According to him, the prince does not only participate in the just war but becomes a part of the just war. He writes, "It is also clear that he who has a just war is not a party, but becomes, by the very reason that impelled him to make war, the judge of his enemies."[97]

In summary, we have seen that Cajetan emphasizes the distinction between offensive and defensive war in order to argue for what he refers to as vindictive justice. For Cajetan, an offensive war, which is also a just war as he has defined it, carries out vindictive punishment against those who have acted iniquitously. Related to vindictive justice are Cajetan's references

90. Ibid.
91. Ibid.
92. Ibid.
93. Ibid.
94. Ibid.
95. Ibid.
96. Ibid.
97. Ibid.

to legal proceedings. This is important because the prince of a just war becomes the judge who gives out punishment. Nonetheless, while the prince may have this right, he is also limited by the actions of the enemy. If the enemy seeks to make satisfaction prior to warring, then the prince is obligated to accept this satisfaction. However, once the war has commenced, the prince is released from the obligation of accepting the enemy's satisfaction.

As we turn our attention to Vitoria we will notice similarities and differences between him and Cajetan. Especially important is Vitoria's consideration of the possibility that a war can be just from both perspectives: the one who is attacking and the one who is attacked. Equally important is the distance that Vitoria seeks to place between himself and Cajetan concerning the idea that a just war could be vindictive.

Francisco Vitoria (1492–1546)

This section focuses on the second part of Vitoria's *relección* in which he discusses the state of affairs in the New World concerning the natives. The first part was delivered in January 1539. The delivery of our current text, *On the Law of War*, may have been strategic in that it was delivered on June 19, 1539, the final day of summer courses at the Universidad de Salamanca. Did Vitoria anticipate the letter that Charles V would send to the San Esteban convent demanding that certain teachings be prohibited and that these documents be destroyed?[98] It would have been a peculiar request, especially during a period in which Spain experienced the free exchange of ideas concerning Spain's presence in the New World. While we may be unsure as to Vitoria's reason for presenting his topic on the last day of the summer term, we do know that he avoided confrontation with his rector concerning the letter from Charles V.

Much has been made of this letter. Does the letter imply a tension between the emperor and the Dominican faculty at the Universidad de Salamanca? Does the letter simply reflect an emperor's desire to control the conversation concerning the New World? Scholars such as Teofilo Urdanoz make the case that Vitoria questioned the actions of the Spanish empire and the letter was in response to that.[99] Others, such as Luciano Pereña, argue that Vitoria failed to question the legitimacy of Spain's presence in

98. Delgado, *Pensamiento*, 42–43.

99. Vitoria, *Obras*, see introduction.

the New World.[100] Finally, there are scholars who maintain that Vitoria tried to justify the expansion of the Spanish empire into the New World. Individuals such as Robert A. Williams Jr., author of *The American Indian in Western Legal Thought*, and the respected Tzvetan Todorov, author of *Conquest of America*, both fall under this category.

It is difficult to reach a substantiated conclusion based on Vitoria's testimony because he fails to address clearly and directly the questions that these scholars have posed. Instead, one is left to consider and reflect on the available circumstantial evidence, which may include direct testimony. The obstacle is not in the circumstantial evidence. Legal scholars have demonstrated the value of circumstantial evidence by appealing to the theory of probability.[101] Of course, this evidence is also weighed against the prejudicial effect of it on those who are hearing the case and will be issuing a verdict. It is possible that the evidence is prejudiced in such a way that it will produce an unfair decision, which is based one something other than reason, i.e., emotions.[102] The issue, then, is how the evidence is presented and whether or not the evidence is prejudicial in nature.

It would seem that the three conclusions that have been drawn concerning Vitoria's relationship to the Spanish empire may be based on prejudicial evidence. Since Vitoria provides no direct testimony of the actual stance he takes, one is left to formulate an opinion that is based on available evidence. Yet, the evidence may be tainted, given that one chooses the evidence based on the prejudicial stance one takes. For example, there is no question as to Todorov's stance concerning Vitoria. He clearly maintains that Vitoria justified Spain's presence in the New World by providing reasons that the emperor could use to defend his stance. Furthermore, Todorov recognizes that his position may be questioned when he makes the case that his position is not related to the Black Legend. In his defense, Todorov states that, "The Spaniards are not worse than the other colonial powers; it just so happens that they are the people who occupied America at the time, and that no other colonizing power has had the opportunity, before or since, to cause the death of so many at once."[103] Aware that his comments could be taken as an extreme position he developed a hierarchy of the Spaniard's responsibility for the natives' death ranging from direct re-

---

100. Luciano Pereña, "Escuela de Salamanca."

101. Bright, *Gruesome*, 184.

102. Ibid.

103. Todorov, *Conquest*, 133.

sponsibility, such as murder, to indirect responsibility, such as introducing foreign microbes that were deadly to the natives. Regardless of the mode in which death occurred, Todorov maintains that the Spaniards are responsible for the deaths of millions in the New World.

At this point it is not prudent to argue whether or not the Spaniards are solely responsible for the deaths of the natives. Instead, the question that needs to be raised is why Todorov only recognizes negative characteristics and motives in the Spaniards. The difficulty with Todorov's perspective is that it assumes that of all Spaniards who were connected to the New World, only Las Casas was interested in issues of human rights. If Todorov is correct when he makes the claim that his position is uninfluenced by the Black Legend, then we must find another definition for the Black Legend because his position is nothing but a denigrating view of Spain and the Spaniards, which is exactly what Julian Juderias had in mind when he made the term popular in his book *La Leyenda Negra*. Todorov's critiques are similar to those found in the writings of individuals such as Francesco Guicciardini (1512–1531), a diplomat from Florence,[104] and Oliver Cromwell (1599–1658).[105] These are individuals are often referred to as chief figures representing attitudes that are characteristic of an anti-Spanish sentiment, i.e, the Black Legend.[106]

Nonetheless, I am not interested in arguing for a specific position that Vitoria takes in reference to the Spanish empire, primarily because this would be difficult to establish unequivocally, even though there is circumstantial evidence that Vitoria challenged Spain's presence in the New World. My interest in considering Francisco Vitoria lies in his methodological approach in addressing imperial power that was well established and unquestioned and in reclaiming a history and sources that have often been unaccounted for and disregarded. In short, I believe that contemporary scholars have much to learn from the likes of Francisco Vitoria. With this in mind, I now wish to turn to Vitoria's consideration of war and how he fits within the history of just war theory that I have presented thus far.

Vitoria organizes his *relección* around three questions. The first question has four parts and includes the issue of pacifism, the authority to go to war, causes of a just war, and the limitations of one's actions in a just war. The second question has to do with doubts concerning the third part of the

104. Guicciardini, "Relacion de Espana," 191–229.

105. Cromwell, *Writings*, 260–64.

106. Gibson, *Black*.

first question—causes of a just war. In the third question he returns to reconsider the fourth part of the first question by focusing on the limitations of war. I will focus on those areas that demonstrate Vitoria's innovative approach to the question of just war.

The first issue that Vitoria takes up is the question of pacifism: Are Christians allowed to defend themselves? He takes up the issue by quoting biblical texts that are often used to substantiate the claim that Christians should resist taking up arms. Included in these texts are Rom 12:19, Matt 5:39, and Matt 26:52, which address the responsibility Christians have to others who are attacking them: they are not to defend themselves, they are not to resist evil. Taking up the sword to fend off attacks implies making oneself vulnerable to the sword itself. At this point Vitoria demonstrates some knowledge of biblical interpretation when he admits, "It is not enough to reply that these words are not precepts, but advice. The objection against warfare would stand, even if wars undertaken by Christians were merely "against the Lord's advice."[107] As we have seen in other areas of Vitoria's writing, he is a scholar who is willing to reach across disciplines and use the knowledge gained to substantiate his point or to respond to the critiques posed by those disciplines. Here, he recognizes that arguing that these texts could be taken as suggestions rather than commands is too simplistic an approach to the question of pacifism.

As is common in the scholastic method, Vitoria presents a counter argument to the biblical texts he has introduced. This argument is based on tradition and authority because it appeals to the "Doctors" of the church and to tradition. Specifically he references Tertullian who, as Vitoria reads him, supported warfare by Christians. On the other hand, Vitoria recognizes that Tertullian at times appears to uphold the position that Christians ought not to go to war.

In addition to referring to Tertullian as someone who may be against war, Vitoria also mentions Martin Luther.[108] Besides using Luther alongside Tertullian as being against war, it is especially important to note that Vitoria was well informed about the circumstances surrounding the Reformation. This knowledge makes Vitoria an ideal candidate to be involved with the Council of Trent, especially when one keeps in mind that the Council was primarily called in order to deal with the Reformation problem. Therefore, it is unnecessary to hold that Charles V was amicable toward Vitoria sim-

---

107. Vtoria, *Obras*, 296.

108. Vitoria, Pagden, and Lawrance, *Vitoria*, 296.

ply because he asked Vitoria to be part of the Spanish commission at the Council of Trent.[109] It is equally plausible that Charles V recognized the best equipped individual to take on the Protestant problem. Regardless of the view one takes, we know that Vitoria was familiar with Luther's writings and had strong negative opinions about the leader of the Protestant Reformation.

Again, following the established scholastic method, Vitoria presents a host of authority figures and arguments that counter the initial claim that Christians are prohibited from going to war. Without reservation Vitoria holds that a Christian may legitimately go to war.[110] Among the authority figures he cites are Augustine and Aquinas. It is unnecessary to go through the arguments of these figures since I have already provided a detailed description of their arguments. Vitoria seems to add nothing new to their positions. Even his appeal to natural law coincides with traditional notions of natural law. His argument is that natural law allowed Abraham to fight against the four kings (Gen 14:14–16).[111] As understood by Vitoria, neither the Mosaic Law nor the evangelical law prohibits natural law.[112]

In this first section Vitoria makes the distinction between offensive war and defensive war. Concerning the latter he maintains there is no doubt in using force for defensive purposes.[113] This distinction will become especially important as he lays out his argument. For the moment we ought to recognize that the distinction he makes between the two is similar to that of Cajetan, but there is a significant difference. For Cajetan, the purpose of offensive war is vindictive in nature. It is about inflicting punishment for a wrong that has been committed.

It is true that Vitoria also considers offensive war as having an aspect of punishment, especially when one is responding to injury.[114] Punishment of the assailant is due because of the injury that was committed. His perspective is, thus far, similar to Cajetan's. However, there is a notable distinction—in the goal of the punishment. For Cajetan, punishment is vindictive in that it is meted out because the assailant committed a wrong. Vitoria, on the other hand, considers punishment as a deterrent to future attacks. He

---

109. Rivera-Pagán, *Violent*, 85.

110. Vitoria, Pagden, and Lawrance, *Vitoria*, 297.

111. Vitoria, *Obras*, 817.

112. Ibid.

113. Ibid.

114. Ibid.

writes, "even defensive war could not conveniently be waged unless there were also vengeance inflicted on the enemy for the injury they have done, or tried to do. Otherwise, without the fear of punishment to deter them from injustice, the enemy would simply grow more bold about invading a second time."[115] Vitoria does not want to punish for the sake of punishing. He is more concerned with the repercussions should there be no offensive war. As he argues, without offensive war, an assailant would continue his attacks. He makes this especially clear when he states, "But there can be no security for the Commonwealth unless its enemies are prevented from injustice by fear of war."[116] It is especially important to note that for Vitoria the "fear of punishment" is enough, whereas for Cajetan the actual punishment is important.

Aligned with the other thinkers I have considered here, Vitoria maintains that war must benefit the commonwealth by providing peace and security.[117] War cannot be conducted for the sake of expanding one's borders, taking another's resources, etc. War must always be for the sake of maintaining the safety and security of the commonwealth/republic. Of course, as just stated, this line of reasoning is nothing new because individuals like Cicero and Augustine already espoused such an idea. What is new in the thought of Vitoria is that what is deemed to be the "good" is expanded beyond the realm of the commonwealth.

For Vitoria offensive war always has a good that benefits the entire world.[118] The "good" that Vitoria has in mind is living without the threat of an other's seeking to take one's belongings.[119] The reason for the offensive war is for the protection of the innocent and to deter future attacks by assailants. Yet, what is innovative in Vitoria is his appeal to the wider world when speaking in terms of good. There may be a hint of this in Cicero when he extends hospitality to those who are outside of his community,[120] but it is Vitoria who widens the good even more by extending it to the entire world.

As I have already argued in chapter 2, scholars usually take Vitoria to task for adhering to an understanding that Höffner refers to as *orbis Christianus*—the notion that only Christians have authority over a specific

115. Vitoria, *Obras*, 817–18; Vitoria, Pagden, and Lawrance, *Vitoria*, 298.

116. Vitoria, Pagden, and Lawrance, *Vitoria*, 298.

117. Vitoria, *Obras*, 818.

118. Ibid.

119. Ibid.

120. Cicero, *Duties*, bk. 1, Sect. 28.

territory. It is unnecessary to revisit the debate on whether or not Vitoria adheres to an *orbis Christianus,* and besides, much depends on how one defines it. If Höffner is correct when he argues that Vitoria maintains that the church plays an important role in the world to the point that he would desire the conversion of the whole world, as well as the church having some kind of legal right over the world, then it would be conceivable to argue that Vitoria functions within an *orbis Christianus.* However, there are two doubts that must be raised. First, it seems that many individuals who critique Vitoria for his "evangelical" stance seem to forget that Vitoria is a theologian and is a member of the Order of Preachers. It would be strange if a Dominican preacher failed to give prominence to the church! Even more strange is the idea that an individual of the Order of Preachers would not want to convert the world to Christianity. This is, after all, understood when one decides to become a member of the Order. It is entirely possible for someone in the Order of Preachers to be uninterested in evangelism, but this would be the exception rather than the rule. Therefore, the critique raised by Höffner seems to be unwarranted.

Concerning the critique that Vitoria is trying to justify the church's juridical oversight of the "gentiles," it too appears to be unsubstantiated. If Höffner has in mind that the church wants to establish its expectations, doctrines, and rituals among those who are converted, then this too is a critique of wanting the church not to act like a church. It would seem that a religious body would want to establish its own rules of conduct. In other words, one must expect the Catholic Church to act like the Catholic Church. Likewise, even within the church various spiritual groups have their own rules of conduct, such as the Rules of St. Benedict. On the other hand, if Höffner wants to argue that Vitoria wanted the church to establish a juridical rule over the unconverted, then this notion would reflect the lack of a close reading of Vitoria's texts.

To buttress the notion that the Church's authority is limited, an idea that is against the *orbis Christianus,* Vitoria concludes that the pope is not the lord of the entire world.[121] To be sure, Vitoria maintains that the pope has spiritual powers on earth, but this is, not surprisingly, limited to spiritual matters. Related to the notion of *orbis Christianus* is the argument that Vitoria wanted to justify Spain's presence in the New World. As Rivera-Pagán states, "One of Vitoria's central objectives is the theoretical

121. Vitoria, *Obras,* 295.

and theological justification for Spanish hegemony over the New World."[122] Rivera-Pagán's claim is based on the fact that Vitoria argued for an economic exchange between the Spaniards and natives. Of course, for Rivera-Pagán this exchange implies that Spain would be the primary beneficiary. Rivera-Pagán has in mind Vitoria's conclusions in *On the Indians*, where Vitoria states, "My first reply is that trade would not have to cease. As I have already explained, the barbarians have a surplus of many things which the Spaniards might exchange for things which they lack."[123] From this text it would appear that Vitoria argues that Spaniards are able to take what they desire from the natives. As understood by Rivera-Pagán, this was Vitoria's goal when he began addressing the native's situation in the *relecciónes*.

Rivera-Pagán's negative approach seems to be based on a preconceived understanding of what Vitoria should have written or lectured about, rather than what he has actually done. Coming from a postcolonial critique of the conquest and Vitoria's position, it appears that Rivera-Pagán has already decided how Vitoria and others should respond to the Spanish occupation of the New World. Vitoria's seem lack of attention to or concern about the welfare of the natives leads Rivera-Pagán to argue for Vitoria's "hegemonic" desire. However, it seems that a healthy dose of respect is needed when considering historical figures such as Vitoria. Historical figures speak for themselves. The task of the scholar is to take the author at face value and deal with her/his ideas regardless of the position.

Furthermore, I suggest that a weakness of Rivera-Pagán's position is the isolation of texts from their wider context. For instance, when Rivera-Pagán makes his economic critique of Vitoria he does so without giving attention to the preceding all-important paragraph in which Vitoria concludes:

> The conclusion of this whole dispute appears to be this: that if all these titles were inapplicable, that is to say if the barbarians gave no just cause for war and did not wish to have Spaniards as princes and so on, the whole Indian expedition and trade would cease, to the great loss of the Spaniards. And this in turn would mean a huge loss to the royal exchequer, which would be intolerable.[124]

Is Vitoria writing prescriptively or descriptively here? If Vitoria is writing prescriptively, then the conclusion would seem to favor Rivera-Pagán's

---

122. Rivera-Pagán, *Violent*, 82.

123 Vitoria, *Obras*, 725; Vitoria, Pagden, and Lawrance, *Vitoria*, 291.

124. Vitoria, *Obras*, 726; Vitoria, Pagden, and Lawrance, *Vitoria*, 291.

position that Vitoria is trying to justify Spain's presence in the new world. However, if Vitoria is writing descriptively, then in addition to critiquing the emperor's stance concerning the issues of the New World by calling into question the justice of the entire expedition and holding the emperor accountable, he is also aware of the political realities of the empire's presence in the New World, i.e., the Spanish will not leave because of the economic benefits; Spain is too invested in the New World and its revenues.

By reading the *relecciónes* closely it appears that Vitoria is not an idealist as Rivera-Pagán argues, "It is the ideal of a Hispanic Christianity that prevails."[125] Instead, Vitoria is a political realist who is painfully aware of the political powers that are at work. In the beginning of *De Los Indios*, Vitoria acknowledges that

> As for the first part, it may first of all be objected that this whole dispute is unprofitable and fatuous, not only for those like us who have no warrant to question or censure that conduct of government in the Indies irrespective of whether or not it is rightly administered, but even for those whose business it is to frame and administer that government.[126]

Here, Vitoria has in mind the initial question that he will be considering in his lecture, which is the right that puts the barbarians under Spanish rule.[127] The decisions to occupy the New World and to incorporate the natives into the Spanish empire had already been made by individuals who had the power to act.

In addition to acknowledging the actual developments of the New World, to question such an expedition would imply that others had not carefully considered their decisions. Yet Vitoria acknowledges that various councils, with its princes and ministers, have considered the legitimacy of Spain in the New World.[128] Vitoria is aware that his immediate influence would be indirect rather than direct because the Spanish Crown was under no obligation to heed his words, suggestions, or advice. Furthermore, the question of whether or not Spain should take possession of the New World is immaterial because they already have possession of the lands and can keep possession without question. Moreover, to raise questions would call into question the aims of the Spanish Crown.

125. Rivera-Pagán, *Violent*, 81.

126 Vitoria, *Obras*, 643; Vitoria, Pagden, and Lawrance, *Vitoria*, 234.

127. Vitoria, *Obras*, 642.

128. Ibid., 643.

Vitoria is aware of the previous thinkers who had considered Spain's presence in the New World. This consideration must, at the very least, give them the benefit of the doubt by allowing the possibility that they were sincere. He refers to the king and queen by their official titles: "Our princes Ferdinand and Isabella, who first occupied the Indies, are known as 'most catholic Monarchs,' and Emperor Charles V is officially titled 'most righteous and Christian prince.'"[129] An interesting point of Pagden's translation is that he inserts the word "titled" when referring to Charles V and translates "cristianisimos" as "most catholic" instead of the more literal and appropriate translation, "most Christian." The difference between Pagden and the original text is that the former makes his translation into titles. Vitoria, however, is not arguing about titles. Vitoria is making an argument about the inner qualities of Spain's rulers. Both Isabel and Ferdinand are "most Christian," and, as such, are assumed to act accordingly. Vitoria does something similar when he refers to Charles V as "most just" and "most religious." These are more than titles. As used by Vitoria, they are adjectives that refer to qualities and characteristics of Charles V.

This distinction is important because if Spain's rulers are the people they are believed to be, then they must act accordingly. It is interesting that the word Vitoria uses to describe Charles V is "most just." Implied is the question of whether or not Charles V really is acting justly. And, if he is not, then Charles V is not just. Vitoria also raises awareness of these qualities because he wants the hearer to understand that any doubts about Spain's presence in the New World is actually a doubt about the character of the most powerful ruler in the known world—Charles V.

Doubt over the emperor's position is raised in particular when Vitoria writes, "Are we to suppose that princes such as these would fail to make the most careful and meticulous inquiries into any matter to do with the security of their estate and conscience, especially one of such importance?"[130] While Vitoria's words seem to indicate there is no reason to call into question Spain's presence in the New World, we must keep in mind that this is exactly what he will do.

Vitoria takes up the issue of Spain's endeavors in the New World because there are doubts about the justice of Spain's ventures. Furthermore,

129. Ibid. "Y ademas, puesto que nuestros principes Isabel y Fernando, que primero ocuparon aquellas regions, fueron cristianisimos, y el emperador Carlos V es justisimo y religiosisimo."; Vitoria, Pagden, and Lawrance, *Vitoria*, 234.

130. Vitoria, *Obras*, 643; Vitoria, Pagden, and Lawrance, *Vitoria*, 234.

Vitoria had already expressed his disgust for the events taking place in the New World. In a letter addressed to Miguel de Arcos, Vitoria writes, "As for the case of Peru, I must tell you, after a lifetime of studies and long experiences, that no business shocks me or embarrasses me more than the corrupt profits and affairs of the Indies."[131] I have already referred to this letter in a previous chapter but it is worthwhile to keep it before us. It appears that not only was Vitoria aware of the abuses and mistreatment that the natives were experiencing at the hands of the Spaniards, he was also distressed and anguished by the actions of his countrymen. Five years later, by the time he began his *relección On the Indians*, the situation in the New World had only become worse. Had Vitoria become uninterested and unsympathetic to what had moved him earlier, or did he continue to be concerned?

We should recall that the letter written to Arcos is dated 1534, which is eight years prior to Las Casas writing his polemical work, *Brevísima relación de la destrucción de las Indias*, published in 1552, six years after Vitoria's death. In short, Vitoria's concern was not dependent on the work of Las Casas, which means there were many others who had raised concerns and that these concerns presumably had reached Vitoria's ears. While we may not know without a doubt whether Vitoria still had the same concerns at the time he wrote the *relección* as were raised in the Arcos letter, we do know that doubts were raised concerning the just endeavors of Spain. The connection between the just nature of Spain's presence in the New World and the unjust treatment of the natives should be obvious, especially when one carefully reads the *relecciónes*, and yet the prominence of this latter matter is ambiguous to some. Rivera-Pagán would have us believe that when Vitoria lectures he no longer has the same interest as he had expressed in the Arcos letter, and that therefore Vitoria is hoping to justify Spain's endeavors—and thus also Spain's cruel treatment of the natives, which had only become worse with the passing of time. This reading, of course, goes directly against what Vitoria wrote to Arcos. I, on the other hand, hold there is some consistency in thought and concern between Vitoria's private letters and his public lectures.

To restate what was set forth at the outset of this project: I am not invested in whether it can be proved without a doubt that Vitoria actually defends the natives rather than justifies Spain's position. Instead, I am interested in the methodological approach that he adopts in addressing events

131. Vitoria, *Obras*, 331.

that have far reaching effects. It is for this reason that I continue my discussion of Vitoria's treatise on just war.

Like many other thinkers who consider just war, Vitoria will take up the question of authority and war by asking who has the authority to declare war?[132] Here, Vitoria is aligned with both Aquinas and Cajetan's questions concerning the authority to wage war. One important contribution he makes is about the role of civil law in justifying the defense of one's property. He writes, "This opinion seems convincing and safe enough, especially as it is supported by civil law; no one can sin by following the authority of the law, for laws justify in the forum of conscience."[133] The issue under consideration is to what extent force is permissible in defending one's property: is it permissible to resist an attacker to the point of taking his life? Vitoria will argue that taking an attacker's life is allowed because failure to do so could result in the loss of honor, which is also an injury. It is important to note that such retaliation is not vengeful, as argued by Cajetan, but rather avoids "shame and disgrace."[134] Vitoria considers the possibility that natural law could prohibit retaliation against the attacker, but is not concerned because civil law allows the retaliation. At issue is not natural law, but that civil law allows such an action. Civil law allows what may be prohibited by natural law.

Vitoria is able to reach the above conclusion because an individual is free from sin when he or she keeps to the law. But what about the uncertainty of conscience? In cases where conscience may be unsure of a particular position to take, civil law becomes the standard by which to evaluate right actions. One should recall that Vitoria is dealing with the justness of retaliating against an attacker to the point that the attacker is killed. His stance is that this type of retaliation is justified; and he finds further justification for this in civil law.

When addressing retaliation, Vitoria backs off from unqualified rhetoric and begins to address restrictions on retaliation. An important aspect of Vitoria's writing, which is often passed over or disregarded, is the frequent inclusion of conditional statements in his treatises. For instance, concerning the current question about the justness of retaliation, Vitoria concludes that retaliation is permissible. Individuals could use such a conclusion to justify Spain's cruel treatment of the natives by arguing that Spain is simply retaliating against threats to her being and property. This

---

132. Ibid., 819; Vitoria, Pagden, and Lawrance, *Vitoria*, 299.

133. Vitoria, *Obras*, 820; Vitoria, Pagden, and Lawrance, *Vitoria*, 300.

134. Phillipson, "Franciscus," 188.

conclusion would be justifiable if the following statement were to be erased from Vitoria's treatise: "And this, I may say, holds true not only for the laity, but also for the clergy and the religious, so long as there is no hint of provocation."[135] The conditional statements force the listener to reconsider retaliation against the natives. There is no one either in the New World or in Spain who would argue that the Spaniards did not provoke the natives into war. In fact, individuals such as Las Casas had already established that the natives were living in peace prior to the arrival of the Spaniards.[136]

The conditional statements added by Vitoria are more than afterthoughts. Instead, they force the careful listener to contemplate what was mentioned prior to the conditional statement. Furthermore, as Vitoria is presenting his arguments the listener would be following along with his conclusions—until Vitoria reached the conditional statement that would serve as a reality check. Rather than agreeing with Rivera-Pagán who argues that Vitoria presents theoretical arguments that are distanced from reality, I suggest that Vitoria presents theoretical arguments that are steeped in the political reality of his day. And it is this reality that is always present in his *relecciónes*, especially those having to do with the natives of the new world.

This is especially evident in the following section where Vitoria turns his attention to consider possible reasons by which a just war could be established. These are mentioned briefly because he has considered them in a previous *relección*, which I have already referenced. He states three reasons for which a just war cannot be established. First, "Difference of religion cannot be a cause of just war."[137] In the previous *relección* Vitoria had already established that the enslavement of the natives could not be justified on the grounds of their rejection of Christianity. He similarly rejects the ideas that expansion of the empire and the glory of the prince are justifiable reasons for a just war. He writes, "Enlargment of empire cannot be a cause of just war."[138] Vitoria's position is further established when he doubts that anyone would consider such a cause as tenable for just war.

The prince does not have unlimited authority to conduct war. Related to this is the argument that the prince cannot wage war justly based on selfish reasons. He writes, "The personal glory or convenience of the prince

135. Vitoria, *Obras*, 820; Vitoria, Pagden, and Lawrance, *Vitoria*, 300.
136. C.f. Casas and Poole, *Defense*.
137. Vitoria, *Obras*, 823; Vitoria, Pagden, and Lawrance, *Vitoria*, 302.
138. Vitoria, *Obras*, 824; Vitoria, Pagden, and Lawrance, *Vitoria*, 303.

is not a cause of just war."[139] At issue here is not the "glory" of the prince, but rather the extent of authority that the prince possesses. Is the prince accountable to someone or something else or is he free to conduct himself as he sees fit? Vitoria will respond to these concerns by adamantly arguing that the prince is accountable for how he uses his authority. According to Vitoria, "The prince must order war and peace for the common good of the commonwealth; he may not appropriate public revenues for his own aggrandisement or convenience, still less expose his subjects to danger."[140] The prince must keep in mind the well-being of the commonwealth because it is to this body that he is accountable. In fact, all authority that the prince exercises is derived from the commonwealth: "The prince has his authority from the commonwealth, and must therefore exercise it for the good of the commonwealth."[141]

The notion that the prince derives his authority from the commonwealth is in direct contrast to the notion of absolute sovereignty developed by Hobbes. For Hobbes, the commonwealth comes into being through submission to either an individual or group that is able to protect the people from one another.[142] It is this submission that gives the prince authority.[143] Furthermore, sovereign authority is without restraints because it is absolute; without this absolute power, "there is no sovereignty at all."[144] Vitoria's consideration of just war is in direct contrast to the Hobbesian approach, which maintains that justness is equated to law; and that a law, by nature, is just.[145] The former considers whether or not the laws are just, i.e., whether there is a higher notion of justness by which the laws are evaluated. Similarly, while Charles V may be the Holy Roman emperor, in Spain he does not exercise absolute sovereignty. Various nobles exercised their own authority over which the emperor had no control.[146] An example of the tension between the emperor and nobles is found during the time when "the electors of Mainz and Saxony" requested Charles to assist them.[147] When Charles announced his intention of going to Germany, the Spaniards balked at the idea that he

139. Vitoria, *Obras*, 824.

140. Ibid.,

141 Ibid.

142. Hobbes, *Leviathan*, xvii.

143. Ibid., xx.

144. Ibid.

145. Elshtain, *Sovereignty*, 107.

146. Philpott, "Sovereignty."

147. Thomas, *Rivers*, 435.

would abandon Spain and leave his affairs in the hands of "foreigners." By way of concession Charles took an oath that pacified Spanish concerns. In turn, "the *cortes* were impressed and voted for the grant of ducats for which Charles had asked."[148] This scenario is representative of the complex role that Charles played in Spain. On the one hand, he was emperor, and was able to exercise all of the rights and benefits of such a role. On the other hand, Charles was economically dependent on the Spanish nobles and recognized that his relationship to them was based on mutual rewards. Charles V was not an absolute sovereign in the Hobbesian sense.

For Vitoria, the prince was indebted to the commonwealth for the authority he received. The prince had the responsibility of making sure that his subjects were not ill-treated. Writing against the idea that war was to benefit the prince, Vitoria notes, "For a prince to abuse his position by forcing his subjects into military service and by imposing taxes on them for the conduct of wars waged for his conscience rather than the public good, is therefore to make his subjects slaves."[149] Vitoria insists that the mistreatment of the subjects for personal gain would make them *de facto* slaves.

Therefore the only reason that justifies warfare is when it is used in response to some injury. "The sole and only just cause for waging war is when harm has been received,"[150] writes Vitoria. This thought is aligned with the history of just war that we have been considering throughout this chapter, particularly as articulated by Augustine and Thomas Aquinas. Similar to them, Vitoria maintains that, "Offensive war is for the avenging of injuries and the admonishment of enemies, as we have seen; but there can be no vengeance where there has not been a culpable offence."[151] Here, Vitoria is similar to previous thinkers when he argues that just war is always in reaction to injury. A nuanced distinction in Vitoria is his insistence that just war cannot be conducted in the absence of injury. While many thinkers would suggest something similar, our author moves beyond a simple statement by emphasizing this condition for just war.

In a departure from his theoretical approach to the question of war, Vitoria brings the issue close to home when he includes himself and his fellow countrymen among those who may carry out a just war. He writes, "It follows from this that *we may not use* the sword against those *who have*

148. Thomas, *Golden*, 34.
149. Vitoria, *Obras*, 825; Vitoria, Pagden, and Lawrance, *Vitoria*, 303.
150. Vitoria, *Obras*, 825.
151. Ibid.

not harmed us; to kill the innocent is prohibited by natural law."[152] Does Vitoria move from the third person because he recognizes the extent of the injuries that Spain has inflicted on the natives in the name of just war? Why does Vitoria drop references to the prince and the figure authorized to conduct just war in the following sections? Has Vitoria forgotten the object of his article?

Answers to the above questions may be beyond our ability simply because we lack any evidence. However, there are some viable explanations for Vitoria's grammatical move. He may be adopting a similar rhetorical device as his counter-part in the New World. When Las Casas writes his *Devastation of the Indies*, he not only writes polemically, but also adopts the third person. Las Casas will always mention the cruel practices of the Spaniards. Of course, he recognized that he was a Spaniard, but he was also trying to get the Spaniards in Spain to speak out on behalf of the natives who were being massacred by the Spaniards. Las Casas appealed to their conscience by making them "guilty" by association.

I suggest Vitoria does something similar. For there is not one Spaniard among his audience who could claim that he had been harmed by the natives of the New World. Furthermore, although Vitoria argues that just war is possible when the injury is loss of honor, no one in the audience could make this claim. Therefore, Vitoria is making a rhetorical and grammatical move that forces the members of the audience (we must remember that his *relecciónes* are lectures that he delivered once or twice a year) to consider themselves addressed.

Another possible reason for Vitoria's grammatical move may be the adoption of a rhetorical device that forces the hearers to reach their own conclusions. A characteristic of this rhetorical approach is that the speaker/author would leave out an important component from the information that is being presented so that the audience has an opportunity to reach their own conclusions by filling in the gaps that the speaker has created. This approach could account for why Vitoria would suddenly include references to the prince in the sections at hand. To be sure, this rhetorical style is meant to be used as an effective tool to communicate one's message rather than being afraid or apprehensive. After all, his audience would have recognized that the natives were the ones who were being injured and harmed by the Spaniards.

---

152. Ibid., 825–26, emphasis mine; Vitoria, Pagden, and Lawrance, *Vitoria*, 304.

It seems that Vitoria leaves open the possibility that the natives may have harmed the Spaniards. Nonetheless, he is quick to state that, "Not every or any injury gives sufficient grounds for waging war."[153] He continues,

> Therefore, since all the effects of war are cruel and horrible—slaughter, fire, devastation—it is not lawful to persecute those responsible for trivial offences by waging war upon them.[154]

Vitoria's position builds on just war thinkers who have argued that war must be proportionate. A difference within Vitoria's thought is his insistence that not all harm or injury requires a response. This view is based on his argument that the reality of war is often disproportionate to the cause. War often takes the lives of innocent victims. Likewise, once war has been commenced against "trivial offences" it is virtually impossible to limit the effects, which are "cruel and horrible."

While the possibility must be considered that the natives injured the Spaniards, there is some doubt as to the extent of the Spaniards' reaction. Returning to his focus on the prince, Vitoria considers what may be done in a just war. Continuing with his argument that a prince may do anything in order to gain peace and security, he appeals to *ius gentium* to argue that the prince has authority not only over his subjects but also over foreigners to keep them from harming others. He writes, "The prince has the authority not only over his own people but also over foreigners to force them to abstain from harming others; this is his right by the law of nations and the authority of the whole world."[155] To be sure, the prince's authority that is being addressed here is that which is gained after a victory. It is not the authority that the prince has over others by right of discovery. It is an important distinction.

This text is pivotal because of the conclusions that other scholars have reached concerning Vitoria's position. For instance, Höffner, an important thinker for Rivera-Pagán's work, argues that Vitoria justified war against the natives on the basis that they were defending the innocent—those who were being offered as human sacrifices.[156] Todorov appeals to Sepulveda's work, *Democrates Alter*, also known as *Democrates Segundo O De Las Justas Causas de La Guerra Contra Los Indios* (*Second Democrates or On the*

---

153. Vitoria, *Obras*, 825–26.

154. Ibid.

155. Ibid., 828; Vitoria, Pagden, and Lawrance, *Vitoria*, 305.

156. Höffner, *Etica*, 439.

Just Causes of War Against the Indians) to establish the argument that the Spaniards justified war against the natives based on their immoral acts. As understood by Todorov, the Spaniards justified their war, "To save from grave perils the numerous innocent mortals whom these barbarians immolated every year placating their gods with human hearts."[157] According to Todorov, it is this one characteristic that justified war against the natives. The problem with this position is that Todorov lumps all Spaniards (including Vitoria) together with Sepulveda and fails to consider debates taking place in Spain concerning the natives. Furthermore, Todorov specifically ignores Sepulveda's complaint that his works had been suppressed by the Universidad de Salamanca prior to his debate with Las Casas.[158] This suppression was due to Vitoria's influence on his students who held two chairs of theology leading up to the 1550–1551 Valladolid debates.[159]

The suppression of Sepulveda's writings is the result of Spaniards' lack of comfort with any arguments that justify the enslavement and cruel treatment of the natives. When taking into account dates of the conquest, the position of Todorov, Höffner, and, by implication, Rivera-Pagán lack evidence. We must recall that Vitoria's *relección* was delivered in 1539. Cortes arrived in the New World in 1517 and had conquered the Aztecs by 1521. All native resistance came to an end by 1533 with Cortes's conquest in Peru. It is hard to imagine any human sacrifices taking place in Mexico especially since Cortes, in November of 1521, had ordered a cross to be placed at the *templo mayor*. In other words, to assume that Vitoria has in mind human sacrifices when he argues that the prince has authority to prevent "foreigners from harming others" is baseless and lacks historical evidence. It is true that in the previous *relección* Vitoria clearly had human sacrifices in mind when he considered a fifth just title by which the Spaniards could take for themselves the natives' possessions.[160] Yet, the delivery of the *relección* was 1537, at least four years after the final suppression of the natives. At most, we can establish that Vitoria is emphasizing the authority of the prince and wants to state that the prince can keep foreigners from harming others.

157. Todorov, *Conquest*, 154.

158. Sepulveda, *Apologia*. Sepulveda complains because he believes that he will not be given a fair hearing in his debate against Las Casas.

159. Hamilton, *Political*, 10.

160. Vitoria, *Obras*, 720.

Who are these foreigners and who are the ones being harmed? Most scholars assume that when Vitoria mentions foreigners he is referring to the natives. But I am not convinced.

Recall that in the first *relección* Vitoria argued that the natives under the law of nations were required to allow the Spaniards to enter their country. The interesting aspect of this section is that Vitoria refers to the natives' land as "their homeland."[161] While the Spaniards are given the right of passage, the land is, nonetheless, the homeland of the natives. It stands to reason that the Spaniards are the foreigners in the land of the natives. Furthermore, in the present *relección* Vitoria argues that following the war, the prince sits as judge between the two commonwealths. He states, "The victor must think of himself as a judge sitting in judgment between two commonwealths, one the injured party and the other the offender."[162] What is interesting about this text that comes at the conclusion of the *relección* is not that the prince sits as judge, which is a different role from Cajetan's notion of the prince as prosecutor, but that Vitoria considers two intact commonwealths and describes them as one being the offender and the other as the injured, though he resists stating which commonwealth is the offender. To be sure, this notion is not similar to what Bartolus referred to as postliminy because the natives were never part of the Roman empire and therefore could not regain their previous lost position. Rather, Vitoria recognizes the independent states of the native republic, but also acknowledges the political reality that Spain is in the New World as a force with which to deal.

Vitoria's *relección* ends by directly addressing the prince. He concludes, "Let him remember above all that for the most part, and especially in wars between Christian commonwealths, it is the princes themselves who are completely to blame; for subjects usually fight in good faith for their princes. And, it is most unjust that, as the poet puts it, the Greeks should suffer for every folly of their kings."[163] Here, he places the blame directly on the prince for all the harm and injury that has taken place in the New World. This is a radical notion in the sixteenth century as in any contemporary moment.

---

161. Vitoria, *Obras*, 707; Vitoria, Pagden, and Lawrance, *Vitoria*, 278.

162. Vitoria, *Obras*, 858; Vitoria, Pagden, and Lawrance, *Vitoria*, 327.

163. Vitoria, *Obras*, 858; Vitoria, Pagden, and Lawrance, *Vitoria*, 327. I have included Pagden's footnote in the translation to capture Vitoria's text as found in Urdanoz's collection of Vitoria's works.

There are few exceptions when Vitoria considers even the possibility that the Spaniards had been injured by the natives. The occasion for the *relección* was due to rumors that the natives were being massacred and robbed of their possessions.[164] Clearly, the injuries of the Spaniards do not serve as the occasion for Vitoria's consideration. To be more precise, Vitoria is concerned with the injuries that the natives have received. This has been covered sufficiently in the previous chapter.

One occasion is when he entertains the idea that the Spaniards are justified for waging war on the natives because they attacked the Spaniards or prevented them from exchanging goods with the natives. Nonetheless, as covered in the third chapter, the conditional statement that the Spaniards could not provoke the natives follows immediately—and this is exactly what had happened in the New World. Therefore, the injured commonwealth is that of the natives mentioned at the conclusion of the *relección* that deals with just war. Furthermore, it is the prince who is to blame for all the harm and injuries that have taken place in the New World.

Throughout this chapter I have been considering how Vitoria fits within the history of just war thought. When he takes up the notion of war in the New World Vitoria is not writing in isolation from this history. Instead, he recognizes previous thinkers and moves beyond their thoughts to address his contemporary situation. As he develops his notion of just war theory, like many other scholars he recognizes that the prince has the authority to conduct just war for the sake of maintaining peace within the commonwealth. War can never be offensive and is always in reaction to an injury or harm. Nonetheless, while the prince may be justified in waging a just war, Vitoria is adamant in stating that not every injury demands war in response, because such an act always brings about the horrors of war. The prince must take every precaution to ensure that the injuries of war are limited. At the same time, however, Vitoria places blame on the prince for every violent act of war in the New World because ultimately he is responsible for the actions of his forces. Therefore, as we noticed in the chapter that considered the *ius gentium*, where Vitoria holds the prince accountable to a higher law, here too he holds the prince accountable.

164. Vitoria, *Obras*, 648.

4

Theology, Authority,
and Coercion

WHILE IT IS DIFFICULT to establish an account of humanism in Spain during the sixteenth century, it is certain that its shape and form were different from what is found in Paris, Italy, and even Germany. The debates and tension between humanists and scholastics in these places may have been, if not absent, then certainly less prominent in the universities of Spain. Moreover, by turning my attention to rhetoric as philosophy I am able to focus on Quintilian to suggest a rhetorical device that was available for Vitoria's use. As I am arguing in this book, Vitoria challenges the emperor's right to be in the New World, but that he does so indirectly. The adoption of this approach is used in order to force listeners to draw their own conclusions concerning the issue at hand. The difficulty in demonstrating that this rhetorical style is in use is that authors will rarely admit using it. Instead, authors assume that the audience has the rational capacity to reach the authors' intended conclusions. In spite of the difficulty involved, I believe that it is possible to show that Vitoria is adopting this rhetorical strategy when he addresses Spain's right to be in the New World. In this chapter I address why he would want to turn to rhetoric. To that end, I situate Vitoria during the time when he delivered the *relección*, highlighting the coercive power of the Spanish rown and Vitoria's relationship to that authority.

I turn first to one of Vitoria's earlier *relecciónes* as a comparison to the current *relección*, *On the Indians*, because both are concerned with individuals who are in power. *On the Indians* is primarily concerned with the emperor's role in and responsibility regarding the cruel treatment of the natives at the hands of the Spanish conquerors. The earlier *relección*, *On Marriage*, is concerned with King Henry VIII's request for the annulment of his marriage to Catherine of Aragon. *On the Indians* and *On Marriage* are ideal comparisons because both address topics that are of concern to individuals with coercive powers. Henry VIII is king of England and not shy about using his position to order the deaths of individuals whom he does not favor. Such is the case of Thomas More who was put to death on July 6, 1535, for treason because he refused to swear the Oath of Supremacy, which recognized Henry VIII as the supreme head of the church. As emperor of Spain, Charles V likewise exercises coercive power. This is especially evident in his affiliation with Clement VII, who succeeded both Leo X and Adrian VI. Clement VII had become uneasy with Charles V's increased power after his defeat of Francis I, who was forced to sign the Peace of Madrid in 1526. When Francis I returned to France, Clement VII incited him to conspire against Charles V. Of course, Charles V was not pleased with such a move and ordered his army to go up against Rome. In 1527 Spanish troops sacked Rome, which may not have been Charles V's intention; nevertheless, it demonstrated that he had and was willing to use coercive power.[1]

I will demonstrate that Vitoria is direct and forceful in his inquiry about Henry VIII's marriage because he is fearless in his confrontations. At the time of his *relección* Vitoria is at the University of Salamanca in Spain and as such is under no threat issued by the king of England. Yet because he is in Spain, Vitoria is exposed to the direct coercive tools of the emperor of Spain. When dealing with Spain's right to be in the New World, Vitoria must adopt a style that seeks to convince the emperor to change in such a way that Charles V will change of his own accord. While this approach is cautious, it is by no means less direct or even less confrontational. Instead, it recognizes those in power and seeks to align them with particular views, but as choices they made rather than being forced by either guilt or otherwise.

Many scholars assume that Vitoria throws his support behind Charles V when it comes to Spain's presence in the New World, reaching these conclusions by comparing Vitoria's writings with those of Las Casas. They are in fact radically different from one another. First, while both Las Casas and Vitoria are Dominicans, members of the Order of Preachers, it is Vitoria who is most dedicated to the scholastic method. This commitment to scholasticism is not uncritical. Vitoria moves beyond the narrowly defined scholasticism critiqued by Martin Luther and many of the humanists of

1. Spahn, "Emperor Charles V."

the sixteenth century by going from a highly rational method of searching for truth to a practical methodological approach of addressing many issues that were of great concern to his contemporaries. Moreover, Vitoria usually takes a rational stance when addressing any topic.

The Polemicist: Las Casas and Spanish Cruelty

In contrast to Vitoria, Las Casas, also a scholastic, resists a completely rational perspective on the topic of injustices in the New World. His resistance to a purely scholastic methodology is especially evident in *The Devastation of the Indies*, where Las Casas is particularly interested in demonstrating the cruelty of the Spanish conquerors by bringing to light practices that would make any modern individual gasp. Rather than scrutinizing the Spanish cruelties through a scholastic methodology, he turns to a polemical style that is dripping with disgust and is often accusatory. For instance, narrating some of the cruelties that the Spanish conquistadores committed in Guatemala, Las Casas states,

> Another incident of unprovoked cruelty was when the Spaniards entered a large and prosperous town no better guarded than another, and in the course of two hours almost destroyed it, putting to the sword men, women, and children and the aged and infirm who could not manage escape.[2]

In this account Las Casas passes over the need to provide his readers with the name of the village that was pillaged and where individuals were put to death by the sword. Unsatisfied with a simple report that states that the Spaniards are acting cruelly, Las Casas gives specific and gruesome details. He writes,

> And the Spaniards have butcher shops where the corpses of Indians are hung up, on display, and someone will come in and say, more or less, "Give me a quarter of that rascal hanging there, to feed my dogs until I can kill another one for them." As if buying a quarter of a hog or other meal.[3]

This image is particularly appalling because the corpses are displayed so that a customer can easily choose the best for his dogs. Not only is one

2. Casas, *Devastation*, 69.
3. Ibid., 128.

appalled that a Spaniard would display these corpses; Las Casas points out that Spaniards purchase the corpses like cuts of meat. The difference here is that the customer is purchasing food for his dogs, food that is part of a human rather than an animal corpse. Notwithstanding the emphasis that Las Casas places on the physical violence, this passage thus also highlights the symbolic and non-physical cruelties committed by the Spaniards.

Las Casas assumes that the natives are as civilized as the Spaniards in Spain, citing as an example the fact that they marry. Las Casas refrains from discussing marriage as a sacrament, and resists the temptation to develop the argument that marriage is a trait of human beings as social creatures. Instead, Las Casas takes for granted that marriage and family life is part of native society. Yet while demonstrating that the natives are similar to all other civilized societies, he makes certain to demonstrate that the Spanish conquistadores have broken marriages and destroyed families.

Las Casas forgoes any discussion concerning the sacramental nature of marriage because the marriages in question took place prior to the natives hearing the Gospel. The Church's notion of marriage as found in Hugh of St. Victor's *On the Sacraments of the Christian Faith*, Peter Lombard's *Book of Sentences*, and Thomas Aquinas's *Summa Theologica* is absent in Las Casas's treatment. As a matter of fact, of the four perspectives concerning marriage identified by John Witte Jr., it appears that Las Casas has in mind only the natural and social views,[4] so he writes of the Spaniards preventing the natives from fulfilling their natural and social ends of marriage.

By presenting the Spaniards as the destroyers of marriages, family life, and society Las Casas implies that they, rather than the natives, are the ones who should be categorized as barbarians. He writes, "The Spaniards broke up marriages, separating husbands and wives, robbed couples of their children, took for themselves the wives and soldiers as consolation, and the sailors bore them away on their vessels that were crowded with Indians, all of them dying of hunger and thirst."[5] While this description ends with deaths due to starvation, the cruel acts that are being focused on are not life-threatening. What is important for Las Casas is that natives' marriages are broken up by Spaniards.

In addition to separating husbands from their wives, Las Casas portrays the Spaniards as barbaric because of their fleshly desires. He writes, "One Spaniard took a maiden by force to commit the sin of the flesh with

---

4. Witte, *Sacrament*, 20–21.

5. Casas, *Devastation of the Indies*, 15.

her, dragging her away from her mother, finally having to unsheath his sword to cut off the woman's hands and when the damsel still resisted they stabbed her to death."[6] Again, by depicting the defenseless nature of the natives, Las Casas highlights the Spaniards' cruelty. Also, the Spaniards' immoral acts are contrasted to the damsel's attempt to maintain her purity, which is especially evident in the young woman's actions even after her hands had been cut off. Las Casas often contrasts the cruelty of the Spaniards with the moral and ordered lives of the natives.

These examples demonstrate the contrasting styles and concerns of Las Casas and Vitoria. On the one hand, Las Casas is especially interested in displaying the cruelties inflicted on the natives to demonstrate the extent of Spanish immorality and injustice. Vitoria, on the other hand, focuses not on specific cruelties but on theoretical questions and unjust practices that affect the natives in the New World.

Without Fear, Without Threat from the Crown

Three years prior to the composition of *De Los Indios*, Vitoria was already aware of the exploitation that was taking place in the New World. As we have already seen, in a letter to Miguel de Arcos, dated November 8, 1534, Vitoria writes, "As for the case of Peru, I must tell you, after a lifetime of studies and long experience, that no business shocks me or embarrasses me more than the corrupt profits and affairs of the Indies."[7] What Vitoria has in mind is what took place following the bloodbath at Cajamarca. Hernando Pizarro had entered Cajamarca and slaughtered the Peruvians along with their leader Atahualpa in 1533.[8] Following the massacre, Pizarro distributed the booty to his men; these, in turn, paid an amount to the royal treasury to legitimize the booty they received, a practice known as compounding. Included in the compounding was an appeal to the papacy.[9] While it may be of great interest to consider whom compounding benefitted, here our interest is on Vitoria's reaction to these practices in the New World. He is both shocked and embarrassed by the actions of the Spaniards who have now returned to Spain to clear their names and ill-gotten gains.

---

6. Casas, *Devastation*, 77.

7. Vitoria, Pagden, and Lawrance, *Vitoria*, 331.

8. Marley, *Wars*, 32.

9. Pidal, "Vitoria y Las Casas," 30–31.

Equally interesting is Vitoria's suggestion for Miguel de Arcos concerning compounding. He writes, "My usual course in such cases is first to run away from them. I do not give [or] take; be sure he has many profits." First, given his comments concerning his "usual course" it is safe to assume this is not the first time he has been asked to give his opinion concerning compounding. Second, I note his desire to put distance between himself and such questions literally by running away from them. When it comes to the issue of compounding he states, "I do not raise my voice 'or beat my breast' against one side or the other until I can no longer pretend."[10] In short, he forfeits any decision concerning the rightness of compounding, but also indicates that avoidance can only be maintained to a certain point, and that when he can no longer withhold judgment, he gives his opinions. Yet, what he offers are not so much judgments but an admission that he does "not understand and can see no safe or just way out of it."[11] At this point, Vitoria will refer the question to "others who understand it better."[12] Yet the evidence in his letter suggests he might be overstating his case when he claims the lack of knowledge to pass judgment. There is some ambiguity when he states he "can no longer pretend." Does he mean he is pretending to have an opinion concerning the case of compounding? If so, that "I merely say I do not understand and can see no safe or just way out of it, and tell them to consult others who understand it better," suggests he has an opinion but is hesitant to make it known. Why the evasion, particularly given the influence and prominence he had in Spain?

Fortunately, we are not left to conjecture the reasons for Vitoria's avoidance of individuals who had to do with compounding. He was quick to denounce unjust actions, and concerned not so much with their tempers but their responses: "some cite the pope and accuse you of heresy for casting doubt on His Holiness' actions," writes Vitoria.[13] "[O]thers cite the emperor and accuse of condemning His Majesty and the conquest of the Indies."[14] There are several especially important aspects here. First, those who are seeking Vitoria's ruling will make their discontent known to both the emperor and the pope. Second, included in this discontent are false accusations that Vitoria is calling into question the authority of both the

10. Vitoria, Pagden, and Lawrance, *Vitoria*, 331.
11. Ibid.
12. Ibid.
13. Ibid.
14. Ibid., 331–32.

pope and the emperor. Finally, Vitoria is well aware of the accusations that are made against him and that these accusations are concerned with the authority of the two most powerful individuals in existence.

There is no indication of whether the accusations that were brought before the pope and emperor happened once or often. Nor is there much indication that Vitoria addressed more than the audience that was concerned with compounding. Yet he was clearly affected by the accusers for he avoided any future cases that dealt with compounding. If Vitoria's private letter to Arcos is any indication of his public attitude, then it is understandable why individuals who had interest in compounding would turn to both pope and emperor. When one continues reading the letter to Arcos it is evident why individuals would turn against Vitoria and make their cases known to both the pope and emperor.

A close reading of Vitoria's letter to Arcos reveals that he adopts a rhetorical stance when challenging the emperor's position concerning the New World. In revealing his position concerning those who are involved in compounding, Vitoria begins by comparing them to individuals who are greedy and interested in monetary gain. These conquerors "may be the type 'that desire to be rich [and fall into temptation]' (1 Tim 6:9), of whom it was said '[it is easier for a camel to go through the eye of a needle than] for a rich man to enter into the kingdom of heaven' (Matt. 19:23–4)."[15] The only motive that Vitoria mentions is that of greed. To justify their greed he argues that they turn to the idea of the law of war. "Here, since the property belongs to someone else," writes Vitoria, "they can allege no title other than the law of war."[16]

This discussion on the law of war, the topic for the second *relección* traditionally referred to as *On the Indians 2*, turns to the subjects of justice, imperial right, and a soldier's duties. Vitoria begins by stating that he does "not understand the justice of the war."[17] This is one of his most remarkable statements, yet Rivera-Pagán, Todorov, and Williams Jr. fail to make any reference to it when they critique his stance on Spain's presence in the New World. To be fair, that reference is in one of his personal letters and not a public lecture. Nonetheless, one should give some attention to his personal letters because, at the very least, they may reveal a tension better hidden there than in the lectures and public presentations. The Arcos letter is dated

15. Ibid., 332.
16. Ibid.
17. Ibid.

three years earlier than *On the Indians*; the earlier letter may demonstrate a tension in Vitoria that may have been resolved by the time he composed the lecture. Whatever the case may be, considering all the evidence does slow one's judgment about Vitoria and even gives him the benefit of the doubt.

Vitoria distinguishes between the justice of the war and the right of the emperor to conquer the New World.[18] On the one hand he states that he does "not dispute the emperor's right to conquer the Indies, which I presuppose he may, most strictly."[19] As we have already noticed in other parts of his writing, Vitoria will state an unconditional case and follow up by providing some kind of restricting clause that will cast some doubt on what he has just stated. One can take for granted that the emperor has the "right to conquer the Indies," yet this right is taken as fact in the strictest interpretations of the emperor's rights. In what sense is the emperor's right to conquer true? Here, Vitoria may have in mind that the emperor's word is the law as stated in the *Digest* 1.4.1. While positive law exists separate and apart from the emperor; only the emperor has the "authority to interpret the law."[20] In the strictest sense, then, the emperor surely has the right to conquer the New World because his understanding and interpretation is law, and, as such, none may question his word. I maintain that Vitoria was fully aware of and accounts for the emperor's authority in his lectures. One should also keep in mind there are two fronts on which the question of the emperor's legal precedence must be taken into account. On the one hand, the emperor has the authority and jurisdiction to change colonial policy, as we see in Charles V's order to release the natives from their *encomiendas* so that they can participate in Las Casas's ideal society.[21] On the other hand, Charles V did not exercise absolute power in Spain. Charles V came to power at the beginning of autonomous nation-states. While I hesitate to recognize an actual nation-state in sixteenth-century Spain, even at that time there were indications of the advent of nation-states. A case in point is the French threat to the New Empire. In 1522, "French ships were observed for the first time off Santo Domingo."[22] Clearly, the French king, Francois I, challenged the authority of Charles V. Moreover, the rebellion of the

18. Ibid.

19. Ibid.

20. Maclean, *Interpretation*, 91. Here, Maclean has in mind the Codex 1.14.1.12.

21. Thomas, *Rivers*, 441.

22. Ibid., 446.

comuneros in 1521 is another example of the struggles that Charles V had to endure in order to exert authority and rule.[23]

It is possible that Vitoria's questioning of the justice of the war against the natives of Peru may constitute a challenge of the emperor's authority. In the case of the Peruvians, his questions rely on the testimony of others, because Vitoria is in Salamanca and has never been to the New World. Nonetheless, the rumors and descriptions of the mistreatment of natives become events that will shape his lectures and *relecciónes* throughout the rest of his career as a theologian. From them he knows that in the "battle with Atahualpa, neither he nor any of his people had ever done the slightest injury to Christians, nor given them the least grounds for making war on them."[24] The "law of war" "justifies" pillaging even from natives who are at peace with the conquerors.

Those who defend the "Peruleros" (those who have taken possessions from the natives and are seeking to justify these actions through compounding) make the case that they were required to "obey and carry out their captains' orders."[25] Yet Vitoria maintains that the soldiers nonetheless have a moral responsibility; they know that the war is motivated solely by greed and therefore should not pillage, even if commanded to do so. Though Rivera-Pagán, Todorov, and Williams Jr. suggest that Vitoria sees nothing wrong in the conquest of the New World, from a brief perusal of Vitoria's personal letters one already finds in Vitoria an attitude that is appalled by the war against Atahualpa and other recent conquests. He recognizes that even within his own order there will be Dominicans who will provide the conquerors "salve [for] their consciences, and even [...] praise their deeds and butchery and pillage."[26] Vitoria is unwilling to compromise on his judgment concerning the wrongness of the wars. He writes,

> Even if I badly wanted the archbishopric of Toledo which is just now vacant and they offered it to me on condition that I signed or swore to the innocence of these Peruvian adventurers, I would certainly not dare to do so. Sooner my tongue and hand wither than say or write a thing so inhuman, so alien to all Christian feeling!

The question remains: Does Vitoria retract or maintain his view concerning unjust Spanish practices in the New World when he presents his

23. Ibid., 446–447.
24. Ibid., 332.
25. Ibid.
26. Ibid., 333.

relección three years later? Should one expect him to maintain the same posture in his public lectures as he does in a personal letter? Or, as I have been arguing, will the public nature of his lectures persuade him to adopt a different stance while maintaining the same level of conviction concerning the unjust practices in the New World? The following section may provide some insights.

As regards the justness of the war against Atahualpa, Vitoria will "grant that all the battles and conquests were good and holy, but we must still consider that this war by the very admission of the Peruvian conquistadors is not against strangers, but against true vassals of the emperor, as if they were natives of Seville." Here he is not saying that the war is justified, only granting this stance for the sake of his next argument, the conquistadors' admission that the natives are the "true vassals of the emperor, as if they were natives of Seville."[27] Furthermore, these same natives are "truly ignorant of the justice of the war, convinced that the Spaniards are tyrannical oppressors waging unjust war on them."[28] Vitoria is considering first, the disclosure by the Spaniards that the natives are vassals of the Spanish empire, and second, the natives' lack of knowledge concerning just war along with their conviction that they are the recipients of tyranny and oppression. The Spaniards are actively involved in the robbery and oppression of the natives, who are merely passive participants and therefore "most certainly innocents in this war," states Vitoria.[29]

The strength of the argument depends entirely on Vitoria's assertion that the current war is good and holy. However, if innocent individuals are the victims of a baseless war, then the entire war should be called into question. This is especially evident when he turns to the emperor's entitlement to wage war. In another conditional statement, Vitoria asserts, "Even if the emperor has just titles to conquer them, the Indians do not and cannot know this."[30] It is necessary to recall that the emperor has authority to interpret law as he sees fit, which would make any understanding of the law the formal and just mode of understanding law. It is equally important to note that Vitoria resists placing the natives under the authority of the emperor. The emperor's entitlement to conquer the natives does not oblige them to accept either his authority or the conditions of his authority. To accept the

27. Ibid., 332.
28. Ibid.
29. Ibid.
30. Ibid.

latter would entail accepting their situation—the conquest of the natives. However, Vitoria asserts that the natives' ignorance precluded any notion of the emperor's entitlement to conquer them, thereby categorizing them as "innocents." Of course, this categorization calls into question the argument that the war is just.

Protector of the Indians—Protected by the Throne: Zumarraga

Before continuing with an examination of Vitoria's *de iure belli* (law of war), I want to consider a strong critique of Vitoria raised shortly after his death by none other than Bartolomé de Las Casas. In the heated debate between Las Casas and Sepulveda, the latter appealed to Francisco Vitoria to prove that the wars against the Indians were justified. True to his passion and zeal, Las Casas turned against Vitoria with the same conviction that he had in defending the Indians against the cruelties of the Spaniards. Commenting on Vitoria's method of composing his *relección*, Las Casas writes,

> Anyone reading both parts of this most learned man's first relection will readily discern that in the first part he proposes, and in a Catholic spirit refutes, the seven claims [there considered] in terms of which a war against the Indians could appear to be just. However, in the second part he introduces eight titles in virtue of which or some of which the Indians might be submitted to the jurisdiction of the Spaniards. In these titles he supposes certain things utterly false, for the most part, that would be required in order that this war be regarded as potentially just—things reported to him by those brigunds who, with complete indifference, are sowing destruction across all that world.[31]

Obviously Las Casas would find Vitoria abhorrent if Vitoria were found to support Sepulveda's position. Las Casas's criticism of Vitoria is based on the notion that entitlements were provided that could place the natives under the jurisdiction of the Spaniards. Similarly, Las Casas maintains that Vitoria's position is based on a lack of knowledge concerning the situation of the New World. Commenting on Las Casas's criticism of Vitoria, the father of Liberation Theology and iconic hero of U.S. Latina/o theologians, Gustavo Gutierrez, writes, "Ignorance of the facts. But also,

31. Quoted in Gutierrez, *Las Casas*, 346.

owing to the credence lent to the oppressors of the Indians, a distorted view of reality. Thus, the eminent doctor's reasoning and suppositions lack any foundation in that reality."[32] In short, Vitoria reached certain conclusions because he was unaware of the concrete situation in the New World.

Las Casas's and Gutierrez's criticisms of Vitoria established the terms according to which scholars have read and studied Vitoria's works. It is unsurprising that such a well-respected scholar as Rivera-Pagán would conclude, "From these questions, with Francisco de Vitoria's help, modern international law was born. It is important to clarify, however, that it is an international law conceived from the perspective of the conquerors, which ultimately served to legitimize armed conquest."[33] He continues his inflammatory remarks against Vitoria by stating, "Many times we forget the markedly bellicose character of the law of nations in Vitoria. It is no accident that his two lectures on the Indians gravitate toward the legitimacy of the objective and methods of the wars against the 'barbarians of the New World.'"[34] Similar to the criticisms of Las Casas and Gutierrez, Rivera-Pagán criticizes the "bellicose character" of Vitoria's texts, but fails to fully explain what he has in mind. From the context of his criticism one would have to assume that he has in mind the critical characteristic of Las Casas's writings. As I demonstrated at the beginning of this section, there is little doubt as to Las Casas's stance concerning the cruelties in the New World. Likewise, Vitoria does not mention any specific cruelties that the natives are experiencing in their persons. Thus for Rivera-Pagán, any language that is not critical like Las Casas's is considered belligerent toward the Indians. In other words, criticism is the key feature of defending human rights.[35] If this is true, then it is expected that Las Casas would be critical of Vitoria.

Both Las Casas and Gutierrez recognize that the emperor of Spain was scrutinizing those individuals who were calling into question the policies that allowed Spain to be in the New World. Presumably this surveillance by the emperor caused Vitoria to write in an indirect way. Disdainful of this "timid" approach and Sepulveda's use of it, Las Casas lashes out against the latter and thereby also the former. Las Casas writes, "Now, as the

32. Ibid., 347.

33. Rivera-Pagán, *Violent*, 201.

34. Ibid., 201–2.

35. During the 2010 SCE International Scholars Program in Chicago, Enrique Dussel mentioned in a personal conversation that the key feature of Liberation Theology and Liberation Philosophy is a critical aspect that is predominantly demonstrated by Bartolomé de Las Casas rather than Francisco Vitoria.

presuppositions of this most learned Father regarding the circumstances are false, and in view of the fact that he says certain things with timidity, in no way ought Sepulveda to have thrown up to me an opinion of Vitoria's that is based on false information."[36] So Las Casas believes that Vitoria has misconstrued certain facts concerning the situation in the New World. But precisely what facts? Perhaps Vitoria's position toward cannibalism in the New World, which Rivera-Pagán argues was the "entitlement" that legitimized Spain's presence. Concerning Vitoria's position, Rivera-Pagán writes, "[he] justified the war against the 'barbarians of the New World' and allowed the 'rights of war' to be exercised against them, one of which was enforced captivity."[37] By taking the side of those who are "innocent" (the victims of cannibalism), Vitoria gives the emperor a legitimate reason (the defense of the innocent) to remain in the New World and even to enslave the natives practicing cannibalism. I will return to this issue when I consider the law of war. For now it is enough to keep in mind that this may be the "entitlement" that Sepulveda envisages when he refers to Vitoria.

The second aspect of Las Casas's accusatory remarks about Vitoria is that Las Casas is primarily concerned with Sepulveda's position and not necessarily Vitoria's. Yet especially in his *Apologia* there are many instances when Las Casas refers to Vitoria in both positive and negative ways.[38] This is not the first time that someone has referred to Vitoria's works in order to substantiate a position. Authors such as Juan Manzano Manzano, Fernando de Armas Medina, and Ramon Jesus Queralto Moreno argue that through his writings and preaching Las Casas produced a "crisis of conscience" in the emperor to the point that he was questioning the legitimacy of his entitlement to the New World. Other authors such as Rivera-Pagán and Gutierrez consider this "crisis of conscience" to be highly doubtful. The term and the discussion about this "crisis of conscience" are based on a document known as "Anonimo de Yucay," which is dated March 16, 1571.[39] Here, the anonymous author makes derogatory remarks toward Las Casas, accusing his diabolical preaching and writings of having created a "crisis of conscience" in the emperor, who was close to withdrawing from the New World. Such a withdrawal would have been accomplished had the Salamancan doctor not intervened with arguments that entitle Spain's presence, as maintained by this

36. Quoted in Gutiérrez, *Las Casas*, 237–38.

37. Rivera-Pagán, *Violent*, 102.

38. Ibid.

39. Salva, *Anónimo*.

document's author. Bataillon presents the most expansive study on the "crisis of conscience" and offers a very convincing argument that the emperor had no intention of abandoning the New World.[40] After his death, various individuals appeal to Vitoria's authority to strengthen their arguments.

What then of Las Casas's comments about Vitoria's "timidity," which came when he and Sepulveda were in the midst of their heated debate that took place in Valladolid in 1550–1551? We know that Sepulveda appealed to Vitoria to establish his argument, and that this caused Las Casas to develop a sharp criticism of Vitoria's writings. What is astonishing about this debate is not the appeal to Vitoria as an authority figure, but rather that the appeal took place four to five years after his 1546 death. Furthermore, the appeal and criticism took place during a period when none of Vitoria's works had yet been published. Indeed, his works were first published by Jacques Boyer in Lyon in 1571, which was an embarrassment to Vitoria's colleagues in Spain.[41] This publication is many years after the Valladolid debate. The question that neither Rivera-Pagán, Gutierrez, Williams Jr., nor Todorov raise is, what text did Las Casas have in mind when he critiqued Vitoria? Of course, a simple reply would be the text of the *relección On the Indians*. However, did Las Casas have before him lecture notes taken by Vitoria's students while he was lecturing? Or, was Las Casas critiquing Vitoria's text as Sepulveda had used these texts? If this is the case, then the critique more accurately is not of Vitoria but rather of Sepulveda's interpretation and use of Victoria's texts. Furthermore, if Las Casas is directly critiquing Vitoria, then from where does he get his information, i.e., texts, since Vitoria himself published nothing during his lifetime?

Las Casas's critique of the Dominican reflects his standard by which all others are evaluated. Yet Las Casas fails to recognize that he was the beneficiary of various privileges that were not available to others, especially Vitoria. First and foremost, as "Protector of the Indians" he in turn was protected by the emperor. From the moment that Cardinal Jimenez de Cisneros appointed Las Casas as "Protector of the Indians" in 1516,[42] Las Casas was able to critique the colonists concerning their harsh treatment of the natives.

---

40. Bataillon, *Estudios*, 344–51.

41. Vitoria, Pagden, and Lawrance, *Vitoria*, xxxiv.

42. Hanke, *Spanish*, 42.

Protector of the Indians:
One of Many

To fully appreciate the reasons why Vitoria would use Quintillian's suggested rhetorical approach, I would like to briefly consider Juan de Zumarraga in the role of the "Protector of the Indians." I have chosen to focus on Zumarraga because there is more information on him as "Protector of the Indians" than there is on Las Casas. I have also chosen Zumarraga because he not only defends the Indians against cruel treatment, but also willfully employs in Mexico all the tools of the Inquisition to maintain a purity of doctrine. His willingness to turn to inquisitorial methods has caused many contemporary scholars and academics to repudiate most of his writings primarily because he fails to measure up to the standard of Las Casas. Yet I maintain that figures such as Zumarraga are an essential part of the Christian tradition; their ambiguity makes historical figures real human beings rather than simply a standard by which one is held accountable.

Juan de Zumarraga was appointed as the Mexican "Protector of the Indians" on January 2, 1528, by Charles V while he was in Spain. As "Protector of the Indians," Zumarraga was to "take under [his] patronage the natives of Spanish America, defending them against the oppression and the mistreatment of the Spanish colonists and whites in general."[43] This statement's lack of clarity and pervasive ambiguity was typical of the difficulties that individuals faced who held this role.[44] Much of the difficulty facing the "Protector of the Indians" did not originate with the Spanish Crown but rather with the new government that was formed in the New World.

The first administrative governmental body was organized in 1511 in Santo Domingo and was established to counter the authority of Diego Columbus. These *audiencias*, as they came to be known, were especially helpful to the Crown in the mainland, but were limited in their influence and importance in the Caribbean. The *audiencia* was organized along the lines of the Spanish Crown and was composed of executive and judicial powers. Each *audiencia* had a president and four *oidores*, judges, who were assisted by legal experts. Usually the President would make decisions with

43. Chauvet, *Fray Juan de Zumarraga*, 284.

44. Bayle, *Protecto*, 41, 59, 70, 71; Fidel de J. Chauvet recognizes two periods concerning the specific duties of the "Protector of the Indians." The first falls between 1517 and 1530, beginning with Las Casas and ending with Zumarraga. The second period begins on August 2, 1530, when the Council of the Indies limited Zumarraga's powers but he did not receive notice of this decision until March 16, 1532.

input from the *oidores*. The first *audiencia* on the mainland was instituted in 1527 as a means of achieving order. The first President was Beltran Nuño de Guzman who was chosen to counter Cortes's authority and power. He was also to investigate charges that were made against Cortes.[45] Unfortunately, de Guzman proved to be a man of low standards and very little character. Rather than investigate the charges against Cortes, "he simply seized his property and Indians, and those of known Cortes supporters, and distributed them among his own backers."[46] Of course, this was only possible because Cortes himself had left New Spain (modern day Mexico) to go to Spain. Prior to going to Spain, Cortes decided to go south in search of a passage into Honduras, and to overpower and execute Cristobal de Olid, who had claimed Honduras for himself. When Cortes reached Honduras, those loyal to him had already assassinated Cristobal de Olid.

When Cortes returned to New Spain, he found a new magistrate, Luis Ponce de Leon, who would be acting governor and would be conducting "an investigation into Cortes's administration since the conquest, and look into various specific accusations, among them assumption of regal privileges, an intention to withdraw the colony from the monarchy, and the possession of excessive rents."[47] The problem was that Ponce de Leon died four days after arriving in New Spain. Some believed that Cortes had poisoned him, but these charges were never substantiated. Rather than seizing his governorship, or claiming himself to be king of New Spain as some of his supporters urged, Cortes decided to lay his case before the emperor himself. Early in 1528 Cortes arrived in Spain and met with Emperor Charles V where he pledged his faithfulness to the crown. He returned to Mexico two and a half years later in 1530. It was during Cortes's presence in Spain that Beltran Nuño de Guzman locked horns with Zumarraga.

I have already noted Guzman's power within the *audiencia* in his taking possession of Cortes's property and Indians. Most scholars of early New Spain would agree that both natives and colonials endured horrific actions at the hands of Guzman, who enslaved Indians and required large tributes from those who had been granted *encomiendas*. But what about Zumarraga's conflict with Guzman? As "Protector of the Indians," Zumarraga was charged with defending the natives from oppression and mistreatment, both of which increased when Guzman became president of the

---

45. Bakewell, *History*, 121.

46. Ibid., 122.

47. Ibid., 115.

audiencia in New Spain. To say the least, the relationship between Zumarraga and Guzman was unstable from the moment that Guzman arrived in New Spain. As understood by Zumarraga, in cases when the *audiencia* was the source of mistreatment of the natives, he possessed the authority to "try them, decide against them and condemn them"; furthermore, he had authority to demand from the guilty rulers themselves unconditional aid in punishing such offenders. The Franciscans welcomed this authority, recognizing that Guzman and the *oidores* were already taking advantage of Cortes's absence (early 1528) by exploiting the natives. With great zeal the Franciscans confronted the *audiencia* through public reprimands and rebukes. Therefore, when Zumarraga presented certification of his appointment, Guzman and the *oidores* recognized and accepted it. But they rejected the delegates—Franciscans already in New Spain—that Zumarraga had chosen, on the basis that their appointment took place prior to the presentation of his documents.[48] Zumarraga's action would continue to be a source of agitation throughout his stay in New Spain.

Immediately following his arrival Zumarraga informed the territory of his duties and authority. In a report to the emperor he wrote,

> I arrived with the four judges, as I have said, at the port of New Spain, and within a short time I published throughout the entire land among all the Spaniards and its natives that I had been sent by Our Majesty as protector and defender of the Indians, and that our majesty had charged me to have special care over those it had and then I got to work to come to this great city of Mexico . . .[49]

Immediately, Indians came to Zumarraga to plead their cases concerning their mistreatment at the hands of the colonialists and the *audiencia*.[50] Many of these complaints included tributes exacted that were above what had previously been set. Concerning those who sought his assistance, he writes,

> At the same time, men from the province of Guasucingo came to me in secret, at that time they were in the encomienda belonging to D. Hernando Cortes, and they mentioned they served D. Hernando as their supervisors ordered, and they provided the tribute as was arranged; and there was a certain time when the president [Guzman] and judges gave them another tribute, and

48. Cheuvet, *Fray Juan de Zumarraga*, 288.

49. Garcia Icazbalceta, *Don Fray*, 1.

50. Ibid., 32.

as if this were not bad enough, they had on a daily basis to take to each judge for his sustenance seven chickens, many quail, and seventy eggs.[51]

Being faithful to this role as Defender and Protector of the Indians, Zumarraga brought these complaints to the *audiencia* and demanded it withdraw the request for additional tribute and treat the men with justice. The *audiencia*, of course, disregarded his demands.

Reacting to his publication and uproar of the natives, the *audiencia* demanded that Zumarraga refrain from interfering with Indian affairs, which was in direct contradiction to his charge, and they barred the Indians from approaching Zumarraga. Anyone who went against these prohibitions would be hanged and any "Spaniard who denounced exploitation of the Indians was to forfeit his property."[52] At issue here is the *audiencia's* attempt to nullify the duties that were given to Zumarraga, attempts that Zumarraga would not survive.

Zumarraga's insistence on defending the rights of the Indians even led him to meet with the president and judges in their homes. It was during one of these visits that Guzman made life-threatening comments against him. Continuing his report to the Emperor Zumárraga writes,

> the president responded to me that they should do what the *Audiencia* order, whether they died or not, and if I sought to defend them, they would punish me the same as the bishop of Zamora was punished.[53]

The Bishop of Zamora was Don Antonio Osorio de Acuña (1459–1526), who had been appointed bishop in 1519. At the time of the Spanish civil war he joined the ranks of the *comuneros* against the throne. He was demoted from his bishopric following a papal bull and given over to the secular authorities who tried, sentenced, and beheaded him. The threat was clearly communicated: if Zumarraga continued his protests against the *audiencia*, his fate would be similar to the bishop. Zumarraga continued with his protests, but this time he took to the pulpit and ordered all the priests under his care to do likewise.

The conflict between Zumarraga and the *audiencia* was not so much a conflict of personalities as a conflict of authority. The *audiencia* believed

51. Ibid.
52. Ibid.
53. Ibid.

that it had received supreme authority from the Crown to do as it wanted. The "Defender of the Indians" recognized the Crown as the origin of his authority but maintained that this authority was over the *audiencia* as well. Zumarraga recognizes the conflict in power and mentions it in his letter to the emperor. Concerning the Audiencia he writes, "and they had ordered me to take into account they were my superiors."[54] The best way to resolve this conflict was to appeal to the emperor himself so that the situation could be clarified, which is exactly what Zumarraga did. He composed several letters to the emperor, but the *audiencia* implemented mail-censorship and blocked any letters that Zumarraga wrote. The extant letter reached the emperor because a shipmate rolled the letter with bacon and then placed it in a barrel of oil so that none of the inspectors could find it.

The result of this protest reaching the emperor is that a new government was set in place in 1530. Two of the judges were removed from their offices and sent to Spain where they died in jail. Guzman, recognizing that Zumarraga was successful in getting a letter out to the emperor, decided in 1529 to go on "an expedition to extend Spanish conquest in western Mexico."[55] However, this expedition may have been more motivated by the fact that news of H. Cortes's return to New Spain was already spreading; he did arrive in New Spain during the summer of 1530.[56] Guzman would eventually die in 1544 in a Spanish prison, in which he had been since 1538.

Several aspects of the conflict between Zumarraga and Guzman throw light on the writings of Francisco Vitoria. First, Zumarraga was commissioned by the Spanish Crown as "Protector of the Indians" and was given special powers over the affairs of New Spain, which had to do with the just treatment of the Indians. Second, while Zumarraga had authority from the emperor he had no coercive power. He had to depend on local authorities to carry out his requests. Third, as Bishop of Mexico, he had an authority that was more persuasive than coercive. The Bishop made use of this influence when he appealed to priests to make protests from the pulpit as he himself had done. Finally, the "Protector of the Indians" had the ultimate authority, the emperor himself, to carry out all duties and requests. While Zumarraga may have struggled to get a letter out of Mexico and have it delivered to the emperor, the full force of his authority came into effect once his letter reached the Spanish crown. Coercion could be exercised as long

54. Ibid.

55. Bakewell, *History*, 122.

56. Ibid., 116.

as the "Protector of the Indians" could get the emperor's sanction, and this would only take place through the hands of the secular authorities.

Francisco Vitoria, unlike Zumarraga, Las Casas, and many others, did not have the title and role of "Protector of the Indians." This difference is especially important because he had to tread lightly when addressing a situation that directly affected the Spanish emperor. Therefore, I contend that when Vitoria speaks in the conditional mode he is not being timid, as Las Casas, Gutierrez, and Rivera-Pagán, would have us believe. Rather, he is employing a tactic that any person would employ who was not sheltered by the role and title of "Protector of the Indians." In other words, Las Casas's boldness is due to his being the "Protector and Defender of the Indians." This does not call into question his genuine concern for the well-being of the natives, nor does it question the passion for justice that he displayed throughout his life. Instead, I simply draw attention to the fact that Las Casas had an underlying reason for being able to speak as boldly as he does throughout his texts. Unlike Las Casas, Vitoria does not enjoy the kind of relationship with the emperor that allows him to speak unconditionally. Vitoria had to be concerned with the coercive power of the emperor. This difference we see in two specific *relecciónes*: *On Marriage* and *On Temperance*.

Coercion Out of Reach

In this section, I return to Henry VIII and his desire to annul his marriage to Catherine of Aragon. More specifically, I am interested in Vitoria's methodological and rhetorical approach to the question of the king's wish for annulment. Already demonstrated above in the case of Thomas More is the king's unequivocal reaction when an individual did not recognize him as the head of the church. Yet, while Henry VIII did exercise immense power, that power was limited to England and its territories and did not include Spain. Moreover, it is nowhere to be found within the walls of the Universidad de Salamanca where Vitoria finds himself. Before turning our attention to Vitoria's *relección On Marriage*, we will consider the circumstances that led up to his public lecture in 1531.

Prince Henry VIII was betrothed to Catherine of Aragon after his brother Prince Arthur was betrothed to Ferdinand and Isabella's daughter, Catherine. The betrothal to Prince Arthur was to ensure positive political relations between England and Spain. Arthur and Catherine of Aragon were married in 1501, but Arthur died in 1502. Trying to maintain peace between England and Spain, Henry VII ensured that Prince Henry VIII, at the age of twelve years old, was betrothed to Catherine in 1503.

The betrothal of Prince Henry and Catherine of Aragon became a legal case that many scholars sought to clarify. First, the case had biblical obstacles that had to be overcome. There are three specific biblical texts that seemingly touch on situations like that of Prince Henry and Catherine. Leviticus 18:16 prohibits a brother from having sexual relations with his sibling's spouse—"You shall not uncover the nakedness of your brother's wife; it is your brother's nakedness."[57] A second biblical passage is located shortly after the above passage and it deals with the consequences should the above circumstance take place in actuality: "If a man takes his brother's wife, it is impurity; he has uncovered his brother's nakedness, they shall be childless."[58] This was especially relevant after King Henry VIII and Catherine of Aragon were wed and she experienced the birth and death of five children, with two who were male and apparent heirs to the throne. The only child who survived was Mary, who was born in 1516. Henry VIII would appeal to Leviticus 20:21 to substantiate the case that his marriage to Catherine was out of alignment with God's purposes and plans for marriage. The third and final text that was relevant to the above case is Deuteronomy 25:5. Here the text states, "When brothers reside together, and one of them dies and has no son, the wife of the deceased shall not be married outside the family to a stranger. Her husband's brother shall go in to her, taking her in marriage, and performing the duty of a husband's brother to her, and the firstborn who she bears shall succeed to the name of the deceased brother, so that his name may not be blotted out of Israel." There seems to be a conflict between these three scriptures, but an apparent resolution is possible when one understands the first two texts to "govern relations when both brothers are alive, and the Deuteronomy passage to govern only after one brother has died."[59]

After the death of Prince Arthur, Catherine of Aragon in 1504 appealed to Pope Julius II for a dispensation to marry Prince Henry. According to Witte, the issue with marrying a brother's widow is one of affinity, which becomes an "impediment to marriage."[60] The pope, however, could wave the dispensation because he was the final interpreter of canon law. In 1527,

---

57. Lev 18:16 NRSV.

58. Lev 20:21.

59. Witte, *Sacrament*, 134–35.

60. Ibid., 135.

Henry VIII would look upon this dispensation as an illegitimate exercise of authority in that the pope ruled against the law of God that was found in the texts from Leviticus. Of course, this appeal was made because he desired a male heir to the throne, and Catherine had already had five "failed" pregnancies, with the only surviving child a female. In the same year, the Archbishop Cardinal Thomas Wolsey conducted a secret trial—*ex officio*.[61]

Henry VIII was accused of going against God's law as stated in the divine law of Leviticus. His defense to this charge was that the pope had granted an illegitimate dispensation, which allowed him to marry Catherine of Aragon. Henry VIII maintained that he wanted to repair his relationship with God by seeking an annulment from his illegitimate marriage to Catherine of Aragon. After doing penance for his violation of the divine law, Witte argues that Henry VIII assumed he would be free to marry a new woman.[62]

Archbishop Wolsey came to realize that the case was more complicated than he imagined. One issue had to do with the extent of his authority and whether the Cardinal's inquisitorial trial could overturn a dispensation issued by a pope. Another was that Catherine of Aragon insisted that she have a say. At the trial she made a claim that would change all the legal ramifications of the case. She maintained that the marriage between her and Prince Arthur was never consummated and that Henry was aware of these circumstances. If this claim was true, then the only obstacle to the marriage would be pride and honesty and not divine law as Henry VIII argued.

Henry VIII's case became more complex on account of his relationships to Mary and Anne Boleyn. The former had previously been his mistress who gave birth to the bastard Henry Fitzroy, yet Henry desired to marry not Mary but Anne. That Henry had already consummated his "marriage" with Mary would be an "impediment of affinity to marrying Mary's sister Anne Boleyn."[63] The contradiction within the cases is too obvious. On the one hand, in the case with Catherine he sought an annulment on the basis that the "impediment of affinity could not be dispensed with," and on the other hand, in the cases of Mary and Anne, Henry argued that the "impediment of affinity must be dispensed with, and permission to

61. Ibid., 136.
62. Ibid.
63. Ibid., 137.

marry must be granted."[64] To muddy the waters even further, the change in popes became an obstacle to Henry's desire to marry Anne.

Clement VII, the newly appointed pope, understood the case that was brought before him by Henry VIII's exponents. However, Clement VII believed himself to be limited in his options. First, Henry VIII had requested a dispensation to be able to marry Anne Boleyn, yet his marriage to Catherine of Aragon was still legitimate. Second, Clement VII faced a political situation that throws light on our current interest in Vitoria. Catherine of Aragon was the aunt of Charles V, Emperor of Spain. Charles V had recently sacked Rome and had been given the title of Holy Roman Emperor by Clement VII. At one point, Catherine demands that the case be moved from England to Rome, which the pope complies with on July 16, 1529. In October of the same year, Clement VII asks Henry VIII to respond to Catherine's claim that she was a virgin at the time of their marriage. No response was given. In March of the following year, Clement VII demanded that Henry VIII stop the planned marriage to Anne Boleyn. After learning that Henry VIII was openly consorting with Anne, the pope threatened the king with excommunication if he did not go back to Catherine. Already in 1529 sides had been sharply marked with "faculties and professors of law" from England, France, and Italy supporting Henry, and faculties from Germany and other European countries supporting the pope.[65] The Universidad de Salamanca would participate in the debate concerning Catherine's marriage to Henry VIII by producing an opinion on the case and sending it, with the approval of the Spanish crown, to the pope. From the *relección* it seems that Vitoria did not participate in putting together the opinion sent to the pope, nor did he necessarily know about the specific contents of the opinion. However, as *prima facie* Professor of Theology, he would often take requests and turn the subject into a course, as Vitoria did on subjects such as simony, homicide, magic, and baptizing infidels. Vitoria also used his contractual obligation to make a public summary of what he had taught during the year, which are some of the *relecciónes* that I have chosen to consider. The *relección* was often different in character and nature to what he had taught in the classroom in that it was a public presentation that was open to all. We are certain that dignitaries and other faculty members, in addition to the regular course attendance of one thousand students, attended the *relección*.[66]

64. Ibid.
65. Ibid., 138.
66. Scott, *Spanish Origin*, 243.

For our purposes, what is interesting is Pope Clement VII's reaction to the above case. First, Clement VII decided to move the trial, as Catherine requested, from England to Rome. Why? Did he simply think it was the right thing to do, or did the fact that Catherine of Aragon was the Holy Roman Emperor's aunt influence his decision? Second, faced with the choice to support Henry VIII, king of England, or Charles V, the Holy Roman Emperor, he opted to throw his support behind the latter. Of course, the recent sack of Rome influenced his choice. If an individual such as Clement VII, who had the power and authority of the papacy, is willing to recognize the superiority of Charles V by choosing to side with the emperor of Spain, then it would make sense that someone like Vitoria, who holds no position of power and authority, would take notice of that regal power. Furthermore, any discussion that questions the authority of the Holy Roman Emperor must be done carefully. Also, when taking on a subject that concerns an individual who has coercive power, one is able to make more direct comments and conclusions if one is oneself beyond the reach of that coercive power. In the following section I consider briefly Vitoria's approach to the question of Henry VIII's marriage to Catherine of Aragon.

As a true scholastic, Vitoria would always present the strongest and best available arguments that were available to his opponents, as he does in this *relección*. He begins by demonstrating the vast resources that are at his disposal by quoting from Cicero's *On Oratory and Orators*. Vitoria uses the story of Hannibal's sarcastic response to Phormio's lecture on the art of battle to demonstrate his uneasiness on speaking on the issue of marriage, about which he has no experience.[67] Yet, at the insistence of his colleagues and students he has taken on the challenge.

According to Vitoria, the basis of his lecture is nothing other than two biblical passages found in Matthew 19 and Mark 10: "what God has united, no man should separate." The *relección* is divided into three parts. He states, "in the first we will deal with the constitution of marriage; in the second, the impediment, and in the third, on the dissolution of marriage."[68] Though I look briefly at the first two sections, my main focus will be on the last section because it is here that Vitoria directly challenges Henry VIII.

Vitoria begins the main body of the text by considering the nature and essence of marriage, which becomes a task of defining marriage. He quotes from Cicero's *On Duties*, "Every study and rational explanation of

67. Cicero, *Oratory*, II. XVIII.
68. Vitoria, *Obras*, 882.

a certain thing must begin with definition."[69] The interesting aspect of his quotation is not that he quotes from Cicero but rather that he quotes from *On Duties,* a philosophical text concerned with ideal moral behavior, which sixteenth-century humanists quoted. Similarly, there is much said about natural law as well as political claims and their connections to moral values. For Vitoria, then, the question about marriage is not simply to define what it is or how to get it annulled. Instead, the question has to do with one's moral standing in the presence of God and those to whom one has an obligation. By asking about the nature and essence of marriage, along with his references to Peter Lombard and the Decretum, Vitoria demonstrates he is familiar with the long history concerning marriage.

Marriage had not always been viewed as a sacrament as the Council of Trent advocated. While the church may have tried to influence the legal ramifications of marriage, it was mostly understood as something secular, being under Roman law.[70] The key component of marriage during the Roman empire was consent.[71] Mutual consent was needed to enter a marriage relationship. This consent could be "between the partners, or between their parents, or whoever had *patria potestas*."[72] Even as the bearing of children was viewed as the purpose of marriage, Ulpian emphasized consent rather than consummation as the essence of marriage. Ulpian writes, "It is not consummation but consent which makes marriages."[73] Elsewhere he would write, "It is not consummation but the intent to get married which makes a marriage."[74] Brooke emphasizes the difference between "consent" (*consensus*) and "intent to get married" (*maritalis affectio*). The former entails a mutual giving between partners as well as families while the latter gives rise to an "aura of sentiment and feeling" that takes place by "slow and delicate stages."[75] Consent was possible at the time of puberty for the male and at "marriageable age" for the female.[76] Brooke maintains that the ages would have been fourteen and twelve, respectively.[77] If this is the case, then we

69. Ibid.

70. Brooke, *Medieval,* 128.

71. Ferguson, *Backgrounds,* 74–75.

72. Ibid.

73 Justinian, *Digest,* 35:1–15.

74. Ibid., 24:1; 32.13.

75. Brooke, *Medieval,* 129.

76. Justinian, *Institutes,* 10.1ff.

77. Brooke, *Medieval,* 137–38.

know why Henry VIII argued that he was too young at the age of twelve to consent to his marriage to Catherine of Aragon. While the purpose of marriage was always the procreation of children, the question that needed clarification was whether consummation was necessary to the essence of marriage.

In the seventh century, St. Etheldreda was married to the king of Northumbria for twelve years and still a virgin.[78] This was her second marriage. Edward the Confessor's marriage had been chaste until his death in 1066. This notion of an unconsummated marriage finds its strongest advocate in the writings of Hugh of St. Victor, especially in *On the Virginity of the Blessed Virgin Mary*. Brooke's translation of a key text follows:

> The two shall become one flesh: this mystery is a profound one, it refers to Christ and the Church; and with delicate logic he says that this must also mean—one soul. After marriage "Henceforth and for ever, each shall be to the other as a same self in all sincere love, all careful solicitude, every kindness of affection, in constant compassion, unflagging consolation, and faithful devotedness . . . Such are the good things of marriage and the happiness of those who love *chaste* [emphasis mine] companionship."[79]

Hugh of St. Victor focuses on a "chaste" marriage with the Blessed Virgin Mary who was married to Joseph in mind. As Ulpian, Hugh of St. Victor makes a distinction between consummation and consent, with the latter being essential to marriage: "It is not consummation but consent which makes marriages." Although an unconsummated marriage as in the case of Mary and Joseph may have been referred to as the perfect marriage, there remained a distinction between choosing to have a relationship which is unconsummated and a marriage where one is unable to consummate the marriage. In the case of impotence, Justinian would allow the annulment of a marriage.[80] He also allowed annulment on the grounds of ascendancy or descendancy, meaning that if the marriage fell within the hierarchy of relations—i.e., father to daughter, mother to son, etc.—then it could be annulled.[81] In the cases of Edward the Confessor and Hugh of St. Victor, we are beginning to see the influence of the church over the definition of marriage.

78. Ibid., 54.
79. Ibid.
80. Ibid., 132.
81. Justinian, *Institutes*, 10.1.

While the church had sought to have partners celebrate their marriage rituals *in facie ecclesiae*—it was not until after the Council of Trent that it became legally necessary to have the ceremony performed within the walls of the church. To be sure, the Council of Florence had already addressed the sacramental nature of marriage in 1431. And in 1208 Innocent IV referred to marriage as being among the sacraments when he wrote against the Waldensians. There is, then, a distinction between marriage as a sacrament and marriage as the ritual that is celebrated in the public view of the church. The earlier notion has a long history going back to the thirteenth century, and maybe even to the early church in the writings of the Apostle Paul. The actual ritual of marriage, the latter view, would become part of canon law after the Council of Trent—long after Vitoria's time.

Returning to Vitoria's idea concerning the essence and nature of marriage, we see that he was aware of the long history and opts to acknowledge that marriage has as its main component the notion of consent. This inference is in contrast to the notion that the essence of marriage is the conjugal rights within the relationship. Vitoria's view is aligned with the two ends of marriage that Aristotle proposes. The first is, "the procreation and the education of children)"[82]; the second, "the help and mutual support between the husband and wife."[83] These ends are based on the idea that the human being is by nature a social animal, and, as such, seeks to propagate and train the children. As a social being, however, the human being is weak. Vitoria states, "Just as man is a weak animal that needs another's assistance, so he is also a social animal."[84] So it would seem that the essence of marriage is consummation. However, as a theologian who is familiar with Roman law, Vitoria brings up an idea similar to Ulpian's: "Is consent between a man and woman the essence of marriage?" writes Vitoria.[85] As understood by Vitoria, consent arises out of the essence of obligation, and obligation is a major aspect of marriage. If obligation exists within a marriage, then it is necessary for the couple to enter the marriage by consent. The necessary conclusion to draw is that consent is the essence of marriage. However, in a typical scholastic form, Vitoria will develop arguments and conclusions that he will later call into question.

---

82. Vitoria, *Obras*, 883.
83. Ibid., 884.
84. Ibid.
85. Ibid., 885.

The reason why marriage must be understood as being more than a relationship of consent and obligation lies in the nature of God. However, Vitoria's ability to write from various perspectives is sometimes difficult to grasp. For instance, James Brown Scott, author of *The Spanish Origin of International Law: Francisco de Vitoria and his Law of Nations*, comes close to viewing Vitoria as a schizophrenic based on Vitoria's various writing styles. Scott refers to Vitoria as the "theologian and jurist, philosopher and humanist."[86] The difficulty with these distinctions is that Scott wants to actually distinguish when Vitoria writes in a specific role—for example, as a jurist and not as a humanist. I, on the other hand, want to acknowledge that Francisco Vitoria is always a theologian who uses the arts, modes, and methods of other disciplines such as law, philosophy, and humanism.

Vitoria understood God as a being who is able to do what God wants and is unlimited by anything, which, to a certain point, includes human freedom. This section on God is a detour from his major goal, which is a discussion of marriage, but it is essential to the text because here he seeks to destroy the notion that marriage is a matter of consent. "God is able to establish that obligation or family ties without their consent, obligating them to a matrimonial union in the same way that they were doing by consent and mutual convenience," states Vitoria. The reason that God is able to do this is because "what [God] is able to do by means of secondary causes, God is able to do God-self."[87] Before we are able to comment on what Vitoria has in mind, we must remind ourselves of what is not meant in this section.

Vitoria is not a nominalist who recognizes a dual power in God. Nominalists would often refer to the *potentia absoluta* and *potentia ordinata* in God, with the former having to do with the ultimate freedom and sovereignty of God.[88] Given God's absolute power there is nothing that God cannot do. The latter notion understands God as having limited God-self so as to be able to do only those things that God has allowed God-self to do. We know that Vitoria is not a nominalist because while he studied at the University of Paris he came under the influence of Peter Crockaert. It is true that Vitoria studied philosophy under the nominalist Juan de Celaya when he arrived at the College of Saint-Jacques in Paris in 1509. Nonetheless, his theological training came under his Thomistic instructor, Peter Crockaert, who had begun to lecture from the *Summa Theologica* rather than from the

86. Scott, *Spanish Origin*, 196.

87. Vitoria, *Obras*, 885.

88. Oberman, *Dawn*, 29.

Sentences, as was the common practice in most universities. Vitoria would follow this practice at Salamanca where he began his professorial duties by lecturing from the *Summa Theologica* II-II.

To best understand what is meant by God being able to accomplish directly what God could do through secondary causes, we recall that Vitoria is a Thomist, and as such, holds that God moves all things. This is similar to Aquinas's notion that God, through grace, moves free will.[89] Yet rather than using the notion of free will to establish his argument, Vitoria will use the idea of dominion.

The reason that God is able to work directly just as God works through secondary causes is because God has and exercises more dominion than God's creature. Vitoria writes, "It is confirmed by the principle that God has more dominion over the man and woman than they have over themselves." He continues, "and if they are able to give over their bodies in what pertains to marriage, God is also able."[90] There is, then, a sense that God is working through secondary causes but is also able to work directly, both of which happen on account of God's dominion.

Vitoria appeals to two biblical texts to support his perspective. The first comes from Hosea 1:1 where God tells Hosea to take a prostitute as his wife and to have children with her. His argument is that the prostitute had little say in her desire to be Hosea's wife, and in this case can demonstrate little dominion over her own body. The same is also true of Hosea since he was likewise commanded by God. What is important is that there is no mention of consent that takes place between Hosea and the woman. A second scripture to which Vitoria appeals is the creation story found in Genesis. Here God commands Adam and Eve to "increase and multiply." Again, Vitoria argues that the text offers no evidence of mutual consent between Adam and Eve, yet they were engaged in a true marriage. From these examples Vitoria will conclude that consent is not essential to marriage.

Nonetheless, he will present counter arguments that will refute these conclusions in the following section. The reason that he finds it necessary to repudiate these is because the implications of the current argument are not sustainable. For instance, as argued by Vitoria, if God is able to bring about marriage without the couple's consent, both the pope and the prince are able to do so too. In the case of the church, she "is able to make one into a monk, and even against one's will; this bond is stronger because it

89. Aquinas, *Summa*, II-II q. 2, art. 9.

90. Vitoria, *Obras*, 886.

invalidates the marriage; then she can also make someone who is single become married."[91] The problem with the church, and the prince, possessing the power to force someone into marriage is that it removes human freedom from the marriage.[92] Vitoria therefore concludes, "I follow the common opinion and affirm that no human authority can establish marriage, but that it requires the consent of the bridegroom and bride."[93] The reason for reaching this conclusion is based on the ends of marriage, which are the procreation of children and their education. Vitoria buttresses this argument by insisting that the ends of marriage requires love because

> without mutual love and conformity of wills, which cannot exist among those who have been forced into union, they are unable to fulfill their obligations, then the spouses are unable to understand and tolerate each other, with each having different thoughts concerning their children.[94]

Where consent is absent, mutual love is impossible; without mutual love, the ends of marriage are impossible to reach. Therefore, for the ends of marriage to be fulfilled consent is necessary.

In the second part of the *relección*, on impediments to marriage, we will begin to see Vitoria's direct address to Henry VIII. The first issue raised by Vitoria deals with the extent of authority of the secular prince. At issue is whether the prince has the same authority as the church to prohibit certain marriages from taking place. This discussion begins by considering the end of civil power, which is the "good of the republic."[95] Since marriage contributes to the well-being of all, the prince can "dictate laws that either impeded or annul a marriage when it is opposed to that good."[96] One should have in mind King Henry VIII's desire to have his marriage annulled and to ask whether he has the power to annul his own marriage. Again, following traditional scholastic methodology, Vitoria will seek to present the strongest arguments for a position that he will seek to dismantle.

In addition to the prince having the responsibility of looking after the common good for the republic, the prince also has the authority to impede what is necessary because of the nature of political prudence, which

91. Ibid., 892.

92. Ibid., 893.

93. Ibid., 894.

94. Ibid.

95. Ibid., 907.

96. Ibid., 908.

all governors and princes maintain in the republic. The prince is able to impede such things as incest, adultery, and rapes through the laws that are established.[97]

A final reason that the prince is able to exercise power over marriages is because marriage is a civil contract. As such, the prince has jurisdiction over it because he has authority over all civil contracts. Furthermore, this jurisdiction is not invalidated by the fact that marriage is a sacrament because the authority of the church does not nullify the authority of the prince.[98]

In his counter argument Vitoria admits that the prince has the authority over marriage in order to prevent family members and relatives from marrying because of his legislative rights.[99] Even so, this authority of the prince was unquestioned and unchallenged prior to the establishment of the church. With Christ a spiritual component to human existence is opened up so that a different set of ends comes to light, to which the secular is unable to direct people; its primary end is the good of the republic, but the higher good is spiritual in nature and needs a spiritual authority to direct people to these ends. Of course, this spiritual authority is nothing other than the Church. Vitoria writes, "I know for certain that the temporal republic is subject in one way or another to the spiritual, and for that matter, the temporal authority is [subject to] to the spiritual."[100] All the same, Vitoria admits that this does not mean that the secular authority is subject to the spiritual in all aspects.[101] There are, however, some aspects of life over which the Church has authority even though the secular authority had enacted related laws.

Vitoria reminds us that marriage depends on "divine right," and it is only by recognizing this divine right that one has knowledge of the rules, standards, and measure of marriage. The secular prince must acknowledge this "divine right" if he is to enact laws that specifically address marriage. As marriage is dependent on the above, it is secular in nature, and, as such, the church has ultimate authority over the affairs that have to do with marriage. Furthermore, this authority over marriage is not based on the sacramental

97. Ibid.
98. Ibid., 912.
99. Ibid., 909–10.
100. Ibid., 912.
101. Ibid.

nature of marriage.[102] Scott is correct when he states, "It is not merely who may legitimately marry; but what authority shall determine the question of legitimacy of marriage."[103] The secular prince is barred from enacting laws that are not aligned with "divine right" and thereby not aligned with the spiritual element of marriage, and he is barred because he does not have the authority to do otherwise.

One can now begin to recognize Vitoria's position concerning Henry VIII's request for annulment from his marriage to Catherine. Vitoria has already limited the authority of Henry VIII by stating that marriage falls within the spiritual realm and not the secular. In contrast to *On the Indians*, this *relección* is direct in that Vitoria specifically mentions that the king is not above the church and must submit to its authority. In the following section, we finally arrive at the point where he mentions King Henry VIII by name and addresses his situation directly by giving attention to the three biblical texts we have considered above.

Vitoria understands the situation between Henry VIII and Catherine as follows: the king argues, "this union was prohibited by divine and natural right; not even the Pope could give a dispensation that would allow him to take his deceased brother's wife as his own, by which the union was and continues to be null."[104] To consider each argument provided by Vitoria would take twice as much space as we have already used. Therefore, I will give a very brief summary of his argument and then go over the main points of his final argument that considers the king's marriage.

Vitoria makes a distinction between those things that are prohibited and those things that are valid because it is possible that the former may actually become valid once they are committed. He writes, "Because many things that are prohibited by human right as much as divine right, once committed, are valid."[105] In providing an example for the former statement Vitoria does not hold back but goes after Henry VIII directly by stating, "with the celebration of a betrothal to a certain woman, divine and human law prohibit one from marrying another woman; but if one does, the marriage is valid."[106] To be sure, he will argue, such an action is against the "law of marriage" but this does invalidate the marriage. At this point he is

102. Ibid., 914–15.
103. Scott, *Spanish Origin*, 251.
104. Ibid., 915.
105. Ibid., 916.
106. Ibid., 917.

willing to accept the argument that the Levitical prohibitions are valid and must be taken into account during his time. He will later state that what is prohibited in the Old Testament is no longer valid under the law of Christ, which is the law of liberty.[107] Certainly this does not imply that everything prohibited in the Old Testament is allowed under Christ: that would be an absurd conclusion. Instead, Vitoria means to state that in cases of negative prohibitions and the absence of it in the new law, one must rely on natural reason and not the prohibitions of the Old Testament.[108]

Turning his attention to the specific question of the marriage between Henry and Catherine, Vitoria considers natural-law prohibitions. At the beginning of this section there is no doubt as to Vitoria's view. He states, "To take in marriage the wife of the deceased brother is not prohibited by natural law."[109] To prove his point he states that actions can relate to natural law in three ways. The first has a positive and negative aspect. The negative aspect of natural law is that there are certain actions that are prohibited and should never be committed, such as adultery and perjury.[110] Correspondingly, there are certain actions that are always "good and conform to reason."[111] Second, there are certain actions that are bad and prohibited by natural law, yet may be legitimate in certain circumstances. Likewise, there may be actions that are allowed by divine right, but would be better not to do. These actions depend on "time, place and persons."[112] The third aspect concerns actions that are not prohibited by "natural right" but are among what Vitoria refers to as "minor goods."[113] Interestingly enough, he will refer to marriage as the minor good compared to celibacy.

After setting the standards by which to measure various acts, Vitoria states outright that Henry VIII's marriage to Catherine does not fall under the first category of actions prohibited by natural law. Vitoria takes this stance because there is nothing explicit that would make the marriage to a deceased brother's wife illicit. Indeed, there is proof that this type of marriage was at one time licit because the deuteronomic text mentions the need to marry the wife of a deceased brother who has no children. Accordingly,

107. Ibid., 921.
108. Ibid., 922.
109. Ibid., 929.
110. Ibid.
111. Ibid.
112. Ibid.
113. Ibid., 930.

it would be "absurd and disrespectful to say that God gave a law contrary to natural right."[114]

In terms of the categories of prohibited actions, Vitoria will deny that Henry VIII's marriage falls under the second. Instead, it is in the third category that he places Henry's marriage. He states that marriage,

> should not be considered as a thing which is bad by nature for any reason is good, but as one of the things that are less good, and, consequently, although not against the natural right to marry the woman's brother, it is not convenient and it is best to refrain from.[115]

One should recall that he has already argued there are certain actions that are prohibited, but once these actions have been carried out they are no longer illicit. The character of discourse at this point is unconditional in nature. The reader is left with no doubt as to Vitoria's stance and opinion. Indeed, when we considered his texts that dealt with the Spanish Crown there was much difference in the discourse in that it was more conditional and the reader was allowed to reach her own conclusions. I maintain that the reason for this difference is that Vitoria is not concerned with the coercive power of a king that resides in England. However, when it comes to Charles V, Vitoria must be especially cautious because the emperor does not have to reach very far to get to him. Using rhetoric, Vitoria lays the case as in a court setting.

Another place that Vitoria mentions the king is in the second principal conclusion of the *relección*. It reads, "Marrying the widow of the brother who died without children, as is the case of the kings of England, was never prohibited by divine right of the old law."[116] This argument seeks to shatter all the arguments presented by King Henry VIII in that it addresses the old law directly. We should recall that the king referred to the texts in Leviticus and argued that the pope should not have given a dispensation for marriage because it was prohibited in the Old Testament. Vitoria will demonstrate that such a position is unsustainable because the text from Deuteronomy allows for the very thing that Henry VIII stated was prohibited.

Vitoria's argument is based on a close reading and interpretation of the texts in Leviticus. He maintains that the texts are not about the widow but have everything to do with children. In seeking to get the texts to coincide

114. Ibid.
115. Ibid., 932.
116. Ibid.

with one another Vitoria will state, "The dispensation is nothing more than the relaxation of the law: and, therefore, it was lawful for each brother in particular to take the wife of his brother who died without children."[117] King Henry VIII, therefore, was within the legal limits of natural law when he married Catherine of Aragon. As such, Vitoria concludes, "that marriage is valid."[118] Again, notice that these final conclusions are without the conditional statements found in Vitoria's other *relecciónes*, and that this difference is due to the proximity of the coercive power of the Spanish emperor and the fact that Vitoria is adopting the court setting where he will present his case.

The Dominion of the Natives and Power of the Emperor

It is tempting to initiate a discussion on the notion of dominion.[119] To be sure, when Vitoria uses the term "dominion" it is used mostly in reference to property ownership as was common in the fourteenth century. Such property law also has its origins in Roman law, as was recognized in the twelfth century.[120] Of course, Vitoria was concerned with the material possessions of the natives in the New World. Even when he delivered his *relección On Civil Power* in 1528 he entirely avoided the term "dominion" and opted for "power." However, when he discusses *On the Power of the Church*, he does use the term "dominion," but this is done only to demonstrate that the pope does not exercise dominion. He writes, "others who think that the pope is lord of the whole world properly by temporal dominion (dominium), and that he has temporal authority and jurisdiction over all princes in the world, are wrong. I have no doubt their view is manifestly false."[121] Neither the civil authority nor the ecclesial authority exercised dominion in the sense John Hus and the Council of Constance suggested. The natives of the New World had dominion in that they exercised property ownership.

117. Ibid., 933.

118. Ibid., 935.

119. The issue of dominion came into prominence with the Council of Constance when it dealt with the heresies of John Hus in 1415. See Ozment, *Age*, 164–72. It should be noted that both Hus and Wycliffe were condemned by the Council of Constance.

120. Coleman, "Property and Poverty," 607–48.

121. Vitoria, Pagden, and Lawrance, *Vitoria*, 84.

Returning to the Council of Constance, one should keep in mind that along with the condemnation of Hus, the Council also condemned Wycliffe.[122] The basis of the condemnation was the supposed anarchy of Hus's and Wycliffe's "teaching on dominion and authority."[123] There are two aspects of Wycliffe's teaching that are especially relevant to our consideration of Vitoria. First, Wycliffe argued that dominion comes directly from God.[124] God, therefore, maintains rights and possession over everything, which means that people do not have possession of things innately. The second aspect of his teaching is that human beings do not maintain dominion over anything. Instead, God gives dominion and ownership to individuals based on their merit. Should an individual live in such a way that is unworthy, then she forfeits all rights to her possessions. This holds true even if positive law and human law would allow the individual to retain dominion. Ozment has reconized that this emphasis, when pushed to its limits, would allow a king to take property away from clergy who were "unworthy." This also allows people to take property away from rulers for the same stated reason.

This brief discussion of the Council of Constance and Wycliffe provides the background for Vitoria's consideration of dominion and property rights. When turning to Vitoria it is necessary to acknowledge there is a change from his earlier writings to his more mature writings that I am considering.

Whether Vitoria is actually defending the natives or whether, as argued by Rivera-Pagán, Todorov, Williams, and even others like Gustavo Gutierrez, Vitoria is mostly interested in providing a rationale for justifying Spain's presence in the New World, becomes clearer when one looks closely at the notion of dominion. In the *relección On the Indians*, Vitoria makes a strong argument that the natives maintain dominion, which Pagden translates as "civil right of ownership."[125] The argument that mortal sin is an impediment to property ownership is destroyed by Vitoria by specifically referring to the Council of Constance, which determined that sin does not negate dominion.[126] Vitoria argues against the conclusion drawn by Almain's commentary on the *Sentences*. Here, Almain argued that a starving man who is forced to steal to survive finds himself in a quandary

122. Ozment, *Age*, 165, 166.
123. Ibid., 170.
124. Ibid., 166.
125. Vitoria, Pagden, and Lawrance, *Vitoria*, 241; Vitoria, *Obras*, 653.
126. Vitoria, Pagden, and Lawrance, *Vitoria*, 241–42; Vitoria, *Obras*, 653–54.

because his robbery, even under the threat of death, remains a mortal sin. This mortal sin would negate dominion in the man who is starving. Vitoria argues that this conclusion is wrong on three counts. First, authors such as Fitzralph (a scholar who argued against Almain's position) and Wyclif have civil dominion and not natural dominion in mind. Second—and the most interesting conclusion when one considers cannibalism—Vitoria argues that in "cases of necessity it is permissible to steal."[127] From Vitoria's words it would seem that mortal sin is not unconditional in terms of law. A certain action may be a mortal sin in one instance but not in another.

At this point I would like to state explicitly what was previously only implied. When Vitoria presents his first *relección* at the University of Salamanca in 1528, he does so in light of the *comunero* revolt of 1520–1521, a revolution that was inspired by the social elites who were fearful they would be forced to cede power and influence to the foreigners who arrived in Spain along with Charles V.[128] Similarly, the peasant's war in Germany had recently been crushed in 1525 with almost 100,000 deaths.[129] Finally, the Protestant Reformation was already underway, albeit in its early stages.

When addressing the issue of civil power, Vitoria does so by speaking in terms of causes. God is to be understood as the efficient cause and the political community as the material cause for the state.[130] As argued by Vitoria, human beings were created with "reason and virtue," which implies that they were created "frail, weak, helpless, and vulnerable . . ."[131] This weakness obligated individuals to live in a society as a way to support one another.[132] The commonwealth, which is the result of human frailty, is "naturally and divinely appointed."[133]

By arguing for the commonwealth's power to compel and coerce right actions for the sake of the common good, Vitoria is appealing to a divine-right theory. He will make this especially unambiguous when he states, "monarchy or kingly power is not only just and legitimate, but also that sovereigns have their power by natural and divine law." Furthermore,

---

127. Vitoria, Pagden, and Lawrance, *Vitoria*, 242; Vitoria, *Obras*, 654.

128. Thomas, *Rivers*, 446–48.

129. Ozment, *Age*, 284.

130. Tierney, *Idea*, 291; Vitoria, Pagden, and Lawrance, *Vitoria*, 6–9; Vitoria, *Obras*, 157–58.

131. Vitoria, *Obras*, 154; Vitoria, Pagden, and Lawrance, *Vitoria*, 7.

132. Vitoria, *Obras*, 154; Vitoria, Pagden, and Lawrance, *Vitoria*, 7.

133. Vitoria, Pagden, and Lawrance, *Vitoria*, 11; Vitoria, *Obras*, 159.

in case there is any doubt, he will add another phrase for the sake of clarifying that the origin of this power is not human. He states that the power to coerce is "not from the commonwealth or from men."[134] As acknowledged by Tierney, Vitoria's conclusion would have gone against prevailing Catholic thought.[135]

In another *relección*, *On the Power of the Church*, delivered four years after *On Civil Power* in 1532, Vitoria will give up on the idea that a ruler receives his power from God. Demonstrating that the power of coercion is not divine Vitoria argues that "princes' power comes wholly from the commonwealth."[136] On what basis does Vitoria change his mind? This is an issue that has disturbed many Vitorian scholars. Unfortunately, there may not be an adequate response for this change. Even Tierney admits the difficulty of clarifying reasons for the change in Vitoria's thought when he writes, "I can see no way to explain the inconsistencies in Vitoria's writings except to assume that the author changed his mind about the origin and nature of the state during the 1530s."[137]

While there are no explicit statements by Vitoria that would account for his change of thought, we are aware of various influences on his thinking. We should recall that the Council of Constance dealt with the issue of dominion by considering the works of John Hus, and especially Wycliffe. We should also recall that the Council was called into session because of the great schism that produced three elected popes that resided in Rome, Avignon, and Pisa. In response to the competing popes, the council flexed its muscles and declared itself "the supreme authority within the church."[138] With the decree *Sacrosancta* (April 15, 1415), we have the beginning (albeit short-lived) of the conciliar theory.

One proponent of conciliarism in the sixteenth century was Jacques Almain (1480–1515). There is evidence that Vitoria knew of and admired Almain. For instance, in his *relección On Dietary Laws* delivered in 1537, Vitoria appeals to Almain to establish a relationship between the political life and virtue.[139] Even as he admired Almain, Vitoria recognized the

---

134. Vitoria, Pagden, and Lawrance, *Vitoria*, 15; Vitoria, *Obras*, 163.

135. Tierney, *Basic*, 294.

136. Vitoria, Pagden, and Lawrance, *Vitoria*, 107; Vitoria, *Obras*, 325.

137. Tierney, *Basic*, 296.

138. Ozment, *Age*, 156.

139. Vitoria, Pagden, and Lawrance, *Vitoria*, 221–22.

implications of Almain's conciliarism. He especially demonstrates this uneasiness with Almain in his *relección On the Indians.*

When he considers the property rights of the natives in the New World and the issue of dominion, Vitoria is especially aware of the actions of the Council of Constance and the teachings of Wycliffe.[140] In defending the natives' property rights, Vitoria argues that sin cannot discount or discredit their dominion because it is "a gift from God."[141] Vitoria makes an explicit reference to Almain when he states, "Almain's argument is invalid."[142]

In addition to appealing to the Council of Constance, Wycliffe, and Almain to develop his notion of dominion and property rights, Vitoria also appeals to anti-conciliar thinkers such as Juan de Torquemada (1388–1468) and Thomas de Vio who later became known as Cajetan (1468–1534). Torquemada, Almain, and Cajetan become significant in light of the early events of the sixteenth century.

A general council was called into session in Pisa in May 1511. This council was the result of a conflict between Pope Julius II and Louis XII of France. The council came together without the express approval of the pope. Naturally, the authority and relevance of the council came to the foreground with the pope appealing to Cajetan to argue against the conciliarist theory that was being espoused by Louis XII. Resulting from the appeal was Cajetan's *De auctoriate Papae et Concilii utraque invicem comparata.* Almain, at the request of Louis XII responded to Cajetan who later wrote another treatise in reaction to Almain. We should keep in mind that while Julius II and Louis XII are in a dispute over the council of Pisa, and while Cajetan and Almain are exchanging treatises, Vitoria is at the University of Paris as a student. As a Dominican student at the University of Paris, Cajetan instructed Vitoria and other students to stay away from the council.[143] When dealing with ecclesiastical authority Vitoria appealed to Cajetan and Torquemada and placed these over and against the Council of Constance and Almain. Specifically, Vitoria positioned himself to make the argument that property rights of the natives are given to them by God. Therefore, they cannot be disregarded even in matters of sin.

In addition to keeping an eye on conciliarism and anti-conciliarism, it is important to recognize in Vitoria a source for high casuistry that will

140. Ibid., 241–42.

141. Ibid., 242.

142. Ibid.

143. Garcia Villoslada, *Universidad*, 174.

be prevalent in the fifteenth and sixteenth centuries, primarily among the Jesuits such as Francisco Suarez who studied at the University of Salamanca and became a Jesuit while enrolled as a student in 1564. It is not surprising that Vitoria would take a casuistic approach, especially given that Cicero, one of Vitoria's major moral and ethical resources, would take a similar approach. In *On Duties*, book III.iv Cicero asks,

> What, then, is it that may sometimes give room for a doubt and seem to call for consideration? It is, I believe, when a question arises as to the character of an action under consideration. For it often happens, owing to exceptional circumstances, that what is accustomed under ordinary circumstances to be considered morally wrong is found not to be morally wrong.[144]

Further along, Cicero will inquire into a rule that allows one to distinguish the "expedient" from that which is "wrong." He writes,

> Some general rule, therefore, should be laid down to enable us to decide without error, whenever what we call the expedient seems to clash with what we feel to be morally right; and, if we follow that rule in comparing courses of conduct, we shall never swerve from the path of duty.[145]

Vitoria withstands the temptation of pursuing a rule what would allow one to determine when stealing would no longer be a mortal sin, besides the general idea of necessity.

Statement of Obligation vs. Denial of Authority

This detour on Vitoria's idea that dominion remains even in the case of mortal sin is especially important because of its connection to cannibalism. Cannibalism had been a major topic in the fifteenth and sixteenth centuries. Individuals from Pope Innocent IV to Montaigne would refer to cannibalism for a variety of reasons. For instance, the former justified the use of arms by Christians against those who practiced the sin of cannibalism. The latter used cannibalism as a template by which Europeans are to view themselves. Montaigne writes,

---

144. Cicero, *Duties,* book III.iv.
145. Ibid.

> I am not sorry that we notice the barbarous horror of such acts, but I am heartily sorry that, judging their faults rightly, we should be so blind to our own. I think there is more barbarity in eating a man alive than in eating him dead; and in tearing by tortures and the rack a body still full of feeling, in roasting a man bit by bit, in having him bitten and mangled by dogs and swine (as we have not only read but seen within fresh memory, not among ancient enemies, but among neighbors and fellow citizens, and what is worse, on the pretext of piety and religion), than in roasting and eating him after he is dead.[146]

Notice that the critique Montaigne raises is on those who judge others with a critical lens and then fail to use that same measure on themselves.

Luis N. Rivera-Pagán may be overstating the case when he writes, "Anthropophagy became the favorite topic of anti-Indian propaganda."[147] Turning his attention to Francisco Vitoria, he states, "It was one of the 'legitimate titles' that, according to Francisco de Vitoria, justified the war against the 'barbarians of the New World' and allowed the 'rights of war' to be exercised against them, one of which was enforced captivity."[148] Rivera-Pagán understands Vitoria to argue that Christians may take up arms in defense of the innocent. The innocent would include those who were being killed in the practice of anthropophagy. In these cases, the emperor is entitled to make war against the natives. To further buttress his argument, Rivera-Pagán turns to Vitoria's *relección On Temperance*, dated 1537 but written for a university course of 1537–1538. Rivera-Pagán quotes Vitoria: "The Christian princes can make war against barbarians because they feed on human flesh."[149] He will conclude his critique of Vitoria by suggesting that the invasion of the New World was sustained through Vitoria's argument. Rivera-Pagán concludes,

> Those natives belonged to a culture that held a worldview the Spanish empire wished to eradicate. That objective probably had greater strategic weight than the humanistic considerations about "the rights of the innocent." The natives, deprived of their cultural and religious values, were ideologically unprotected from

---

146. Montaigne, *Montaigne's Essays*, 155.

147. Rivera-Pagán, *Violent*, 102.

148. Ibid.

149. Ibid.

the invader, who imposed the rules of the game and proceeded to enslave anyone who did not follow them.[150]

Further he will state, "It [Vitoria's view] managed to convert a bellicose invasion into a redemptive action."[151] Without Vitoria, according to Rivera-Pagán, the invasion of the New World never would have been justified and viewed as a just war.

The issue I have with Rivera-Pagán is not with his use of Vitoria, for Vitoria does argue on behalf of the innocent by stating that those with power ought to come to the defense of those who are unable to defend themselves. Rather, the issue is that Rivera-Pagán fails to situate Vitoria when appealing to his writings. Furthermore, he never takes on the difficult case of those who were in reality being sacrificed and eaten. In other words, Rivera-Pagán is especially concerned with those who were overthrown by the power and might of the Spanish empire. But should he not also be concerned with those individuals who were carried off by the Aztecs and offered up as human sacrifices? Does empire only do that which is unjust, or can it also act on behalf of justice? Is the Aztec empire any less innocent simply because it has been defeated by the Spaniards? What does one do with the fact that Spain never could have won a single battle in the New World had it not been for those tribes and nations that were the vassals of greater empires such as the Aztec? Is it possible that Rivera-Pagán himself has succumbed to a "colonial discourse" that makes it difficult to recognize goods in an empire?

Turning our attention to Vitoria, I want to state clearly that I am not trying to defend Vitoria as the great defender of the Indian, although he may be exactly this. I am more interested in learning from his insights. Unfortunately, when one develops preconceived conclusions—e.g., that all Spaniards, with the exception of Las Casas, were only interested in justifying the Spanish conquest of the New World—it makes it almost impossible to learn from scholars in the past. Furthermore, when one views Las Casas as the only champion of justice in the New World, one only gets half of the story that is taking place in the Spanish empire during the sixteenth century.

When considering the *relección On Temperance*, we should keep in mind that it was written in 1537, three years after Vitoria's personal letter to Arcos but also two years prior to *On the Indians* (January 1539) and two and a half years before his text *On Just War* (June 1539). When compared

150. Ibid., 103.
151. Ibid.

to the later texts one must keep in mind that the former may be a more immature text in which Vitoria has not yet fully developed his position. Clarification is in order.

It is true as Rivera-Pagán stated that Vitoria maintains that the Christian prince may take up arms to defend those who are subject to anthropophagy. Vitoria writes, "Hence, since it is a fact that these barbarians kill innocent men, at least for sacrifice, princes may wage war on them to force them to give up these rituals."[152] The justification for such an action is not that natural law has been violated but rather that, "they involve injustice to other men."[153] Rivera-Pagán will argue against the distinction that Vitoria makes between natural law and justice, per se. Rivera-Pagán sees human sacrifice as being contrary to justice as argued by Vitoria, but also contrary to natural law because such sacrifice is "mortally harmful for the innocent."[154] I am unconvinced of the merit of arguing that human sacrifice is contrary to natural law, especially since such a conclusion is not as clear as Rivera-Pagán may have in mind. Recall that Vitoria has stated that in cases of necessity a mortal sin may not be a mortal sin.

The problem with Rivera-Pagán is that it appears as though he is anticipating the conclusion that he wants to reach when he reads texts from Vitoria; if he had only kept reading *On Temperance* he might have been more hesitant in his conclusions. The text that we have just considered, and which Rivera-Pagán quotes, comes from Question 1, Article 5: "Is it lawful to make war on the barbarians if they practice anthropophagy and human sacrifice? Fifth conclusion: Christian princes can declare war on the barbarians because they feed on human flesh and because they practice human sacrifice." The following conclusion should have made Rivera-Pagán hesitate. Vitoria writes, "Sixth conclusion: If war is declared on the barbarians by this title, it is not lawful to continue once the cause ceases, nor to seize their goods or their lands on this pretext."[155] He then strengthens his position:

> I assume that, even if the war is fought by just title, the belligerent does not thereby have the power to eject the enemy from their dominion and despoil them of their property at whim; he can act

---

152. Vitoria, Pagden, and Lawrance, *Vitoria*, 225.

153. Ibid.

154. Rivera-Pagán, *Violent*, 103.

155 Ibid., 226.

only as far as is necessary to ward off injustices and secure safety for the future.[156]

A conditional statement follows that could have been used by Rivera-Pagán to strengthen his conclusion:

> It follows that, if there is no other method of ensuring safety except by setting up Christian princes over them, this too will be lawful, as far as necessary to secure that end.[157]

From Rivera-Pagán's perspective, Vitoria is establishing the basis for the justification, or "redemptive action," of Spain's presence in the New World. Of course, it is also possible that Vitoria may be establishing the standard by which the "Christian prince" can be appraised.

The following conclusions reached by Vitoria seem to limit the rights and actions of the emperor in the New World rather than establish a *carte blanche* for the Spaniards. For instance, Vitoria compares the rights of the prince to go to war with the natives to the rights that the prince has to make war with other believers:

> It follows that, just as a Christian prince having just cause for war against another Christian does not immediately gain the right to depose the other from his princedom, so in the present discussion of a war against barbarians there is no immediate right to despoil them of their lordship and properties.[158]

One of the issues that both Vitoria and Las Casas had in common was the protection of the native's dominion and property. On the one hand, Las Casas will seek justice by attacking the *conquistadores* far removed from the coercive power of the emperor. On the other hand, Vitoria will place a greater responsibility on the duties and actions of the emperor. And, this is where I maintain that Vitoria has adopted the court setting for his presentation. However, in this current *relección*, he appears to be addressing the emperor directly because his conditional statements are not as frequent as in subsequent *relecciónes*. Rather than directly challenge the Emperor's authority, Vitoria holds him accountable to the ideals he holds. Vitoria states in clear terms the obligations of a Christian emperor. Of course, the implication of what Vitoria writes could be that the emperor is not acting

156. Ibid.
157. Ibid.
158. Ibid., 227.

like a Christian emperor, which would have been out of line for Charles V, the "Holy Roman Emperor."

Similar to Las Casas, who is seeking to establish better living conditions for the natives by addressing the abuses of the *encomenderos*, Vitoria seeks to make the natives' condition better by addressing the one individual who has the right and power to bring about change in terms of the law. He argues that the Christian prince, in addition to the promulgation of just laws, must ensure that the individuals who are given the task execute just laws. Concerning the laws, Vitoria writes, "a prince who obtains sovereignty over [individuals] is obliged to make suitable laws for their commonwealth also in temporal matters, so that their temporal goods are protected and increased, and they are not despoiled of their wealth and gold."[159] This text is especially interesting in that it addresses the subject of gold, which is of great importance to the emperor. The emperor, according the Vitoria, is to restrain from taking gold out of the New World. He writes, "It follows from this that if it is in the interests of that commonwealth to prevent the export of gold out of the kingdom, the prince would do wrong to allow it."[160] "This is clear from what has been said above, and confirmed by analogy: if the king were to permit gold to be exported from Spain to Italy, he would act wrongly." He continues, "The same must therefore hold of the Indies, in the absence of any other reasonable cause."[161] Rather than taking from the Indies, the emperor is to make certain that the natives are not deprived.

Vitoria concludes the *relección* by summarizing his previous arguments, which should come as no surprise. What is surprising is the absence of a previous argument, specifically the argument attested to by Rivera-Pagán. Vitoria's main concern in the conclusion is toleration: ". . . although a legitimate prince may enact laws to abolish the unbelief and rituals of pagans and to introduce Christianity, this must be done reasonably and in a tolerable manner, without undue violence or oppressive measures against the subject," he writes. He will turn to the specific issue of cannibalism by stating,

> Finally, where they say that they can be punished for 'sins against nature,' what do they mean: specifically sins against the natural order and against instinct such as sodomy and anthropophagy, or generally sins of any kind against natural law?[162]

159. Ibid., 227.
160. Ibid., 228.
161. Ibid.
162. Ibid., 230.

If his opponents are concerned with specific sins, then, he maintains, it is possible "that unbelievers can be convinced just as well, or indeed better, of the evil of murder or perjury as they can of the evil of sodomy." However, if his opponents have general sins against natural law in mind, then Vitoria recognizes that certain individuals are simply trying to justify the mistreatment of the natives. He writes, "But if our opponents use the term in the general sense, of any sin against natural law, this is nothing more than a fraudulent calumny concocted to justify persecuting non-Christians."[163] He will even recognize that these individuals are not necessarily concerned with sin, but simply want to make war against the natives. "They may as well say it is lawful to wage war on all unbelievers and be done with it," he states. Vitoria is, therefore, more worried about the abuses that could take place in the New World than he is about defending the innocent people who are being offered up as human sacrifices.

From this brief observation of a few of Vitoria's texts, we have concluded that his approach to a particular topic is dramatically different when there is no threat of coercion. As we discovered in his *On Marriage*, he takes a direct approach when he concludes that King Henry VIII is unable to get an annulment from his marriage to Catherine of Aragon. This direct approach is even evident in the other *relección* that we have considered, *On Temperance*. The reason for his direct and unconditional statements is because Vitoria does not have to worry about coercion, since he is not calling into question the emperor's authority or power. Instead, he is addressing the responsibilities and obligations of a Christian prince who is concerned with being a good prince. When we get to *On the Law of War* in the next section, we will see a dramatic change in his approach. First, Vitoria will subject the emperor to the same law, *ius gentium*, as all others. In other words, the emperor does not have a special or different relationship to the law of nations, nor is the emperor in a position to interpret the law of nations for himself. Instead, the emperor is accountable to the commonwealth for acting justly. Furthermore, if the emperor does not subject himself to the law of nations, there is, then, some question as to the legitimacy of the emperor's rule. This assertion was just as radical in the sixteenth century as it is in the twenty-first century.

If one is going to question the emperor's authority, it would be prudent to consider how to do so. Second, in contrast to the "Protector of the Indians," who has the protection and support of the coercive power of the

163. Ibid.

emperor against the ruling governors, judges, and *audiencias*, in the New World, Vitoria does not have any coercive power to protect him. In fact, Vitoria's relationship to the coercive powers is, at best, ambiguous as we have demonstrated from his letter to Arcos. Already, Vitoria had been accused of questioning the authority of the emperor and the pope. There were people like Martin Luther who were willing to question the authority of the pope. However, would Luther have been equally bold in his claims against the pope if he had not had the support of Frederick III, Elector of Saxony, who asked for Luther's examination to take place in Augsburg?[164] One must be circumspect when one questions the imperial authority of the only coercive power that is within reach of oneself.

164. Oberman, *Luther*, 192–97.

5

Spain, Humanism,
and Vitoria

HAVING ESTABLISHED A LEGAL history of the conquest of the New World in chapter 1, and having considered some of Vitoria's texts, the setting and context of such texts, as well as the structure of his arguments, it is appropriate to briefly consider why Vitoria would have adopted the argumentative structures as he did. Of course, in this consideration it is necessary to consider how humanism influenced the work of Francisco Vitoria. This task proves somewhat difficult in light of the fact that he rarely, if at all, makes references to humanism in his works.

Equally difficult in demonstrating the relation between Vitoria and humanism is his location. Apart from the time he was in Paris for his education, Vitoria spent all his time in Spain at the University of Valladolid and the University of Salamanca. Due to the Black Legend, which shapes a preconception of Spain's status, it is often difficult to demonstrate the positive aspects that have come out of Spain. Again, this is by no means to deny the cruelty and violence that the natives suffered at the hands of the Spaniards who arrived in the New World. My goal is to recover a history that is positive and that reaches beyond Las Casas, and may even extend further into the past to the likes of Cicero, Seneca, Boethius, and others.

Aligned with my overall goal, the purpose of this chapter is not to prove without a doubt that Francisco Vitoria was a humanist. Instead, I am mostly interested in the similarities between humanistic concerns and those of Vitoria. For instance, both are interested in the moral character of their audience. In the case of the latter, he is interested in the Emperor's disposition. The issue to be addressed at this point is whether or not Vitoria was directly influenced by humanism in his concern over the character of the emperor. This proves to be a difficult task to undertake due to the perceived role of humanism in Spain.

There is a consensus among many scholars that humanism failed to take root in sixteenth-century Spain. The role of humanism in places like France, Italy, and even Germany is evident;[1] the tension between humanists and scholastics can be easily discerned at the universities of these respective countries.[2] When one turns to Spain, however, the aura is different. With the establishment of the University of Alcala by Cardinal Jimenez, there is intentionality in advancing humanistic endeavors.[3] There is even evidence that Cardinal Jimenez tried to get Erasmus to participate in the Complutensian Polyglot.[4] Of course, Erasmus never accepted this invitation. These examples represent the presence of humanism in Spain. Yet, the overwhelming conclusion about humanism in Spain is that it is absent. This idea has its beginnings in the work of Gil Fernandez who argued "there is no humanism in Spain."[5] Of course, when considering Fernandez's work it is important to understand that by humanism he has in mind, "the actual cultivation of classical studies and, more specifically, the teaching of classical languages and literature in modern Spain."[6] Regardless of Fernandez's definition of humanism, what is important is his influence on the attitudes of many scholars who study sixteenth-century Spain, which results in a negative assessment of Spain.

At the other end of the spectrum are works similar to Ottavio Camillo, who has an extremely positive opinion of Spanish humanism in the sixteenth century.[7] Somewhere between the pessimistic view of Fernandez and the optimistic view of Camillo lies a more realistic view of humanism in sixteenth-century Spain. For the purposes of this project I will only be considering that more realistic aspect of humanism as it relates to and influences Francisco Vitoria.

Contributing also to a negative view of Spain and humanism are individuals such as Juan de Valdes, who studied at the University of Alcala

1. Kristeller, *Medieval*, 6–8.

2. Rummel, *Humanist-Scholastic*, see especially chapter 4.

3. Rummel, *Jimenez*, 53–57.

4. Ibid., 61.

5. Gonzalez, *Escuela*, 9.

6. Camillo, "Interpretations," 1193.

7. Fernandez Lopez, "Rhetorical," 139.

and authored *Dialogo del Mercurio Y Caron*, in which he attacks the corruptions of the Catholic Church. Fearing the Spanish Inquisition, he left for Naples in 1530. His comment that only Italians were able to master the Latin language was made over and against his fellow Spaniards, which would eventually contribute to a negative view of the presence of humanism in Spain.[8] The attitude of Valdes has, unfortunately, become common among scholars. A case in point is Anthony Pagden's claim in his introduction to Vitoria's texts. Arguing against Beltran de Heredia's position that Vitoria brought together in his works both "Thomism and Christian Humanism," Pagden maintains that Vitoria completely rejected humanism.[9] To substantiate his claim Pagden refers to Vitoria's comments that he had sinned by spending much time studying the natural sciences and humanities. Unfortunately, Pagden fails to consider what Vitoria had in mind when he refers to the humanities. As such, it is necessary to consider what Vitoria has in mind when he regrets having studied the "disciplines of the Greeks," i.e., the humanities.

Humanism and Scholasticsm

Charles G. Nauert Jr. summarizes the controversy between humanism and scholasticism when he writes, "In a general way, most (but not all) of these appear to be confrontations between education and church-reform proposals of the humanists, on the one hand and, on the other hand, the established academic and ecclesiastical authorities, especially the scholastic theologians and the religious orders."[10] In general, humanists had an aversion to scholasticism because the former believed that the latter had little regard for historical integrity. Scholastics often viewed humanists as mingling in affairs for which they lacked any training. Their fields of expertise included "grammar, rhetoric, poetry, history, and the study of Greek and Latin authors,"[11] yet, this limitation did not keep humanism from influencing other fields such as medicine, philosophy, law, and theology. Of course, experts in these latter fields would consider humanists who directed their

---

8. Camillo, "Interpretations," 1198.

9. Vitoria, Pagden, and Lawrance, *Vitoria*, xiv.

10. Nauert, "Clash of Humanists," 1.

11. Kristeller, *Renaissance*, 101.

writings outside of their fields as trespassers, or amateurs at best.[12] This intrusion not only led to conflicts between scholastic and humanistic personalities, but also contributed to rivalries between the well-established chairs and authorities at prominent universities and the comparatively new humanists. Nonetheless, the conflict between scholastics and humanists was more profound than simply being a difference between personalities, and an intrusion of foreigners into an academic field not their own.

The fundamental source of conflict between the humanists and scholastics was that of method.[13] The older and well established discipline of scholasticism was dedicated to a dialectical method; scholars would consider a thesis and an opposing thesis, and then seek to arrive at a conclusion based on the theses. Peter Lombard's *Sentences* is an example of a typical approach within the theological field that many, if not all, universities used in the fifteenth and sixteenth centuries. Humanists, on the other hand, were more interested in the sources and historical particularity.[14] The different methodological approaches of scholastics and humanists are especially evident in the field of law. For example, Guillaume Bude (1467–1540) is associated with the *mos gallicus*, the new humanistic approach to legal studies that includes a critique of the organization of the Justinian *Code*, and opposed to the *mos italicus*, associated with the postglossators and the well-established approach to legal studies in the fifteenth century.[15]

Another methodological point of contention between the humanists and scholastics was the role of the *Quaestio*. Important genres for scholastics included the "textbook, the commentary, the *Quaestio*, and the treatise," while the humanists focused on "textbooks, commentaries, and treatises."[16] The distinction between the two is the role of the *Quaestio*. For scholastics, the *Quaestio* was second only to the commentary. In the twelth century, structural change took place within scholasticism, and Kristeller writes about the resulting new style in which "a proposition is laid out, then arguments which support it are presented, then some counter-arguments, and finally counterarguments are refuted and the proposition thereby declared as proven."[17] Essential in this framework was the place of the dispu-

---

12. Nauert, "Clash of Humanists," 12.

13. Ibid., 13.

14. Franklin, *Jean Bodin*, 23.

15. Maclean, *Interpretation*, 14–16.

16. Kristeller, *Renaissance*, 5.

17. Ibid., 8.

tation as related to the *Quaestio*. The *Quaestio* would lend itself to authority figures debating/disputing over a particular question or statement that had been set forth.[18] The disputation would often last over a two day period. Of course, the goal of the disputations was to reach truth.[19]

For the humanists, in contrast to the scholastics, the *Quaestio* was omitted, which "reflects antipathy to the disputation."[20] Instead of having a dialectical analysis as common among the scholastics, the humanists would emphasize, "Grammatical and historical interpretation."[21] In general, humanists were more interested in style, rather than "terminology" as with scholastics.[22]

In addition to the difference of method, Erika Rummel identifies three further features that contributed to the conflict between scholastics and humanists. First, there is the "natural resistance to change," that scholastics would have developed.[23] Individuals who were comfortable with the academic status quo would become perturbed with the approaches that the humanists advocated. Second, there was the "fear of pagan contamination."[24] Due to their interests in classical authors such as Cicero, humanists were accused of supporting pagan morality, which was viewed as corrupt.[25] Finally, Rummel suggests that the conflict between scholastics and humanists was augmented by the latter's "rejection of sophisticated language."

Such general analyses of the scholastic-humanistic debate unfortunately develop dichotomies. Both scholasticism and humanisms are presented as spheres that are exclusive of one another. Yet, as Kristeller has argued, scholasticism and humanism were not necessarily opposed to one another, and the conflict between the scholastics and humanists is often overstated.[26] In other words, scholastics did not reject all humanistic features; rather, they often adapted these features to their own agenda. Likewise, humanists did not reject scholasticism outright. A case in point is Pico della Mirandola, who argued contra Ermolao Barbaro's counsel,

18. Baldwin, *Scholastic*, 61.

19. Ibid., 75.

20. Kristeller, *Renaissance*, 10.

21. Ibid.

22. Ibid.

23. Rummel, "Et Cum," 719.

24. Ibid., 720.

25. Ibid.

26. Kristeller, *Renaissance*, 100.

"against study of the uncouth dialectic."[27] There is, then, the possibility that humanism and scholasticism are able to coincide, especially when an individual addresses a concern that is of interest to both disciplines, an approach central to humanism.

Ernesto Grassi and Humanism

An important work in this regard is Ernesto Grassi's *Rhetoric as Philosophy: The Humanist Tradition*, in which Grassi attempts to overcome the overly rational Cartesian speculation that is derivative of scholasticism. To accomplish this Grassi recovers the humanistic tradition by demonstrating the differences within humanism that considers rhetoric in a philosophical manner and that branch of humanism that is identified along the lines of rationality. Grassi is concerned with maintaining the unity of *res* and *verba*, "content" and "form," which is similar to what is found within the Latin tradition.[28] Grassi's critique of Descartes is that he split the union of "content" and "form" by advocating for the "rational element" alone. According to Grassi, Descartes' emphasis is the epitome of the scholastic movement. Unfortunately, Grassi's alignment of Descartes' "split" with scholasticism puts the latter under negative light; it distorts one's evaluation of the scholastics in the sixteenth century who are assumed to be uninterested in the union of *res* and *verba*. While humanists of the sixteenth century were adamantly critical of rational speculation employed by many scholastics, scholasticism itself underwent a transformation that is particularly evident at the University of Salamanca in the person of Vitoria. However, the unity of *res* and *verba* that Grassi is interested in maintaining is found in his summary of Quintilian.[29]

Grassi's focus on Quintilian is important for several reasons. First, Quintilian, along with Aristotle and Cicero, becomes especially influential in sixteenth-century Spain.[30] Second, while there has been much emphasis on the works of Aristotle and Cicero,[31] Quintilian is virtually unknown

---

27. Nauert, "Humanism as Method," 430.

28. Grassi, *Rhetoric*, 35–37.

29. Ibid., 46–52.

30. Fernandez Lopez, "Rhetorical," 145.

31. Nunez Gonzalez, *Ciceronianismo*, 103–23.

among religious circles, and yet his works figure prominently in Spain.[32] Therefore, by referring to Quintilian I will indicate how the neo-scholastics of the school of Salamanca, and Vitoria in particular, were aware of and incorporated rhetoric as a philosophy into their theological enterprise and concern for human rights.

Grassi argues that the Italian humanists, as grammarians, maintain the union of *res* and *verba*, which is accomplished in Quintilian's connections between the object and verb in grammar. As a professor of literature Grassi is especially interested in the task of grammar. His discussion of grammar follows his discussion of Quintilian's unity of *res* and *verba*, which gives the impression that this unity is only found in grammar. A closer look at Quintilian, however, reveals a different reading of *res* and *verba* unity.

Quintilian's discussion of the object-verb relationship is found in *Inst. Orat.* 1.4, 18 and *Inst. Orat.* 1.5, 2. This is followed with a consideration of the different types of speeches that include the legal, political, and eulogistic speeches.[33] The legal and political speeches are found within the courts of law. Instead of addressing the three different types of speeches, Quintilian will speak in terms of causes, which include judicial causes and extrajudicial causes. The eulogistic speech is identified with the latter cause.[34] This allows Quintilian to address how the audiences are affected by the speeches rather than addressing the types of speeches. The audiences are those who seek to be gratified, to be counseled, or who seek to form a judgment.[35] Rather than drawing attention to the judicial causes, Grassi bypasses them by focusing only on the extrajudicial causes that have gratification as their goal.

The dilemma with Grassi is not that he places emphasis on the poetic, but rather that this emphasis is at the expense of the disunity of the orator. According to Quintilian, the orator can be both rhetorician and philosopher.[36] The true orator is one who is concerned with and able to combine morals, science, and eloquence. This combination is what is found in many of the writings coming out of the University of Salamanca, particularly those by Francisco Vitoria, Domingo de Soto, and the highly honored jurist Diego de Covarrubia y Leyva, known as the "Spanish Bartolus." Following

---

32. Hernandorena, "Presencia de Quintiliano," 1162–79.

33. Quintilian *Institutio*, 3.4, 1–8.

34. Ibid., 3.4, 6.

35. Ibid.

36. Ibid., preface, 13.

Quintilian, they understood that legal speech provides more than an actual case, but rather allows the emergence of the *quaestionis,* which Grassi also recognized. What Grassi failed to concede is that the *quaestio* is a fundamental element of scholasticism. Scholastics such as Vitoria recognized the importance of the question, yet the *quaestio* does more than raise questions about a case. It raises suspicion about the entire case. As Grassi recognizes, "The legal 'matter' hence does not consist of a mute 'existing' state of affairs, but of the entire questionableness of the respective case."[37] I will address Quintilian further when I consider the rhetorical arguments that Vitoria may be presenting.

Spain and Humanism

While humanism became of interest to individuals in Spain as in other European countries, unsurprisingly, Spanish humanism developed its own "distinguishing characteristics."[38] As with Italian and French humanism, Spanish humanism reflected its specific cultural characteristics, including a strong nationalism that would extend to New Spain in the form of language, particularly through Antonio de Nebrija's (1441–1522) composition of the first grammatical work of any of the romance languages.[39] After completing his education in Italy, Nebrija obtained the professorship of poetry and grammar at the Universidad de Salamanca. Later, he would leave Salamanca and join the Universidad de Alcala de Henares at the request of Cardinal Jimenez de Cisneros.

Cardinal Jimenez de Cisneros commissioned the new university to become a central institution for the study of humanism. The orientation of the Universidad de Alcala de Henares was determined by theology. While Scholasticism was still prevalent at Alcala, here we are interested mostly in its use of the Bible in studying original languages and the use of Thomas Aquinas's *Summa Theologica* rather than the traditional *Sentences* of Peter Lombard. This latter practice was begun by Peter Crockaert in 1512 at the University of Paris. Crockaert used the *Summa* as the basis of his lectures rather than "the required text in all the universites in the middle ages which continued into the early sixteenth century."[40] A student of Crockaert,

37. Grassi, *Rhetoric,* 49.

38. Bono, *Cultural,* 19.

39. Nebrija, *Gramatica.*

40. Garcia Villoslada, *Universidad,* 279, translation mine.

Francisco de Vitoria would, of course, continue and make popular the practice of using texts of Aquinas in his public lectures. There is, then, in the Universidad de Alcala de Henares an assortment of both humanistic and scholastic interests. However, one does not need to go to the newly founded University of Alcala to find the amalgamation of the above disciplines.

Students at the Universidad de Salamanca would have to participate in various exercises at important stages in their academic careers. Before becoming professor of canon and civil law, Diego de Covarrubias y Leyva (1512–1577), "author of ten widely read volumes of legal commentaries; advisor to Charles V and Philip II; Bishop of Ciudad Rodrigo from 1560–1565; Bishop of Segovia from 1565–1577; and President of the Council of Castile from 1572–1577,"[41] employs the use of humanistic traits in his orations. Included in these are the use of pagan authors, such as Cicero and Horace.[42] At the Universidad de Salamanca, probably the greatest scholastic center in the sixteenth century, the use of humanism is obvious.

Law and Humanism

As a science with its own body of literature to be studied and commented upon, the study of law was first developed at the University of Bologna in the eleventh century.[43] There are three elements that Berman identifies that allowed the study of law to blossom.[44] First, the discovery of the Justinian *Code*, which Justinian I ordered to be compiled between 529–534. This body of literature came be known as the *Corpus Juris Civilis* (Body of Civil Law). Second, the scholastic method provided a framework for considering the *Corpus Juris Civilis* in a manageable way. Finally, the development of legal disciplines in various universities allowed the study of law to continue.

The robust connection between the scholastic method and the study of law is immediately obvious. At the University of Bologna, the text used for instructing students in law was the Roman law, which contained four separate parts. The first was the *Code* and contained the decisions of Roman emperors prior to Justinian. The second part was the *Novels*, which was a composition of laws promulgated by Emperor Justin himself. A short

41. Liere, "Humanism and Scholasticism," 2.

42. Ibid., 6.

43. Berman, *Law and Revolution*, 120–21.

44. Ibid., 123.

introduction to the study of law for beginning law students composed the third part of the Roman law. Finally, the last part, the *Digest*, contained the decisions and opinions of various Roman jurists. It was the *Digest* that became the part of Roman law that was considered and studied the most.

The principal tool for considering the massive body of jurists' decisions was scholasticism. It provided an analysis of and conclusions about the massive amount of decisions found in the *Digest*, many of which were in conflict with one another.[45] Eventually, glosses began to be amassed in the *Digest*. These glosses often neglected questions of historicity.

This neglect of history became the fodder for the new method that humanists championed and which was dominant throughout the fifteenth and sixteenth centuries. Guillaume Bude's (1467–1540) publication of *Annotationes in Pandectas* in 1508 became one of the first sustained attacks against the jurisprudence of the medieval age.[46] Using humanistic ideals, Bude approaches medieval jurisprudence as a misinterpretation of the Roman Law. Of course, this approach would eventually turn its critical eye to the scholastic method that sought to make sense of the large number of jurist decisions found in the *Digest*.[47] Humanists maintained that scholastics lacked sufficient Roman legal history to understand Roman law, which was historically particular. This latter charge weakened the notion that Roman law was universal;[48] and indeed the French never accepted Roman law as universal and binding on all peoples.[49] The new methodological approach of the humanists allowed suspicion concerning the legitimacy of Roman law as common law for France to continue.

In summary, humanists questioned the legitimacy of scholasticism in understanding and interpreting Roman law because they disregarded historical particularity of the *Digest* and other sources that were used. Furthermore, the legitimacy of Roman law as a universal law was called into question because Roman law was considered to be promulgated at a specific place and time in history. If it was promulgated as a particular law, then its suitability to places and times other than that specific setting was dubbed as illegitimate. In short, Roman law lacked the force of law when applied outside the setting where it was promulgated.

45. Ibid., 132.

46. Franklin, *Jean Bodin*, 18.

47. Ibid., 20.

48. Ibid., 23.

49. Ibid., 37.

Vitoria and Humanism

Francisco de Vitoria was born in Spain either in 1485 or 1492–93, shortly after Columbus discovered the New World; he died on August 12, 1546.[50] At the age of 13, Vitoria entered the Dominican monastery in San Pablo de Burgos and became known as an aspiring humanist. In 1510, Vitoria moved to Paris to continue his studies at the University of Paris in the Dominican College of James or Saint-Jacques.[51] It is here that Vitoria came under the influence of Peter Crockaert, a nominalist-trained professor who rejected his training by studying and teaching Thomas Aquinas rather than the more conventional Peter Lombard's *Sentence*. Vitoria would follow suit at the University of Salamanca, where he was elected to the Prime Chair of Theology in 1526, lecturing on the *Summa Theologiae* rather than on the *Sentences*.

Vitoria delivered his lectures *De Los Indios* in 1538–39 (during the then-prime teaching hour of 6:00 am, which reflects the honor that was given to the prima chair) as a way to fulfill his duty of offering a public reading, known as *relección*.[52] In view of the public nature of this reading, it is no surprise that Carlos I (Carlos V, Holy Roman Emperor) would prohibit the publication of *De Los Indios* until 1557.[53]

According to Ricardo Villoslada, it is possible that Guillaume Bude and Francisco Vitoria were both at the University of Paris at the time when Vitoria was studying.[54] If so, then it is possible that Vitoria heard Bude lecture. Regardless of whether or not Vitoria attended Bude's lectures, we are positive that Vitoria heard of Bude and understood the new learning that Bude was advocating. Vitoria referred to Bude as an impious heretic[55]— not for using a humanistic method (grammar) for studying the Bible, but for using humanistic methods to the exclusion of theology. This criticism should come as no surprise, especially when one considers the high view that Vitoria has of theology. The role of a theologian, for Vitoria, is "The office and calling of a theologian is so wide, that no argument or controversy

---

50. Pagden dates Vitoria's birth in 1485 but Teofilio Urdanoz places Vitoria's birth following the discovery of the new world. Vitoria, Pagden, and Lawrance, *Vitoria*; Vitoria, *Obras*, 5.

51. Vitoria, *Obras*, 9.

52. Scott and Vitoria, *Spanish Origin*, 73.

53. Williams, *American Indian*.

54. Garcia Villoslada, *Universidad*, 329.

55. Heredia, *Manuscritos*, 52–54.

on any subject can be considered foreign to his profession."[56] A theologian ought to be able to discuss any issue from a theological perspective. And, when a humanist, who is not trained in theology, uses grammar to study the Bible without reference to theology, he is prone to follow the path of impropriety.

When discussing any issue that has to do with law, Vitoria always refers to the *Summa Theologica*. This is especially true when he discusses Roman law. Actually, the only real reference that Vitoria makes to Roman law is when he refers to *ius gentium* in the Justinian *Code*. However, the reference to the Justinian *Code* is quickly supplanted when he turns his attention to Thomas Aquinas's passing reference to *ius gentium*.

Vitoria maintains an ambiguous relationship to the champions of humanism. For instance, Renaudet has documented the influence of Erasmus and even Juan Luis Vives on the writings of Vitoria.[57] Yet, there is some question as to the extent of a direct influence on our thinker. While we do know that Vitoria came in contact with both Erasmus and Juan Luis Vives during his time at the University of Paris, we are unaware of any extended exchanges among these individuals.[58] There is evidence, however, of Erasmus's attempt to contact Vitoria when the Spanish Inquisition decides to judge the works of Erasmus.[59]

Erasmus is aware that the accusations being brought against him are due to a perceived connection he has to the Reformation, specifically an association with Martin Luther. According to Erasmus, these accusations are sustained by Diego de Vitoria, who is Francisco Vitoria's brother.[60] In the letter to the latter, Erasmus states that he is not worried about Diego and Francisco being brothers because he is sure that Francisco will be on the side of truth. Likewise, Erasmus defends himself against any perceptions that he is against scholasticism.[61] An interesting aspect of this reference is that while Erasmus states he is not against scholasticism, he does not mention that he is supportive of it. Indeed, though he mentions being involved

---

56. Vitoria, Pagden, and Lawrance, *Vitoria*, 3; Vitoria, *Obras*, 150.

57. Renaudet, *Préréforme*, 406, 408, 467.

58. McKenna, "Francisco," 639.

59. Garcia Villoslada, *Universidad*, 346.

60. Ibid., 347.

61. Ibid. "I am not condemning scholasticism . . . The world expects from us something excellent and something superhuman [above human]."

in working on "something excellent," he does not unequivocally connect this to scholasticism.

There is no evidence that Francisco Vitoria received the letter from Erasmus. It appears from the references to the Sorbonne that he believed that Vitoria was still in Paris whereas in fact he was at the University of Salamanca. The most noteworthy feature of the letter is that while Erasmus is coming under suspicion he believes that he has an ally in Vitoria. Whether this belief is due to Vitoria's relationship with his brother or because Erasmus recognizes that Vitoria has just accepted the Prima Facia Chair in Theology at the University of Salamanca, thereby giving him a place of influence, we are unsure. What is certain is that Erasmus is confident that Vitoria will take his side. If this is the case, then Erasmus should have known that he had many allies is Spain.

In 1527 the Spanish Inquisition gathered theologians to consider the orthodoxy of the works of Erasmus.[62] Among this group is our very own Francisco Vitoria. It appears that the Assembly was called to respond to the publication of the *Enchiridion* in Spanish. The Inquisitor General Manrique was forced by the monastic orders to call together the Assembly both to arrange and categorize their accusations against Erasmus, and as a means of keeping Erasmus out of the public eye (the Inquisitor General reminds the monastic order that they are prohibited from accusing Erasmus in public).[63]

Of the twenty charges that were made against Erasmus only two were actually considered by the Assembly in Valladolid. The first deals with the *comma Johanneum*, which was the primary text (1 John 5:7) used to combat Arianism. In his translation Erasmus had left it out because it was not found in any Greek manuscripts. He would eventually put the text back in another edition, but this did not satisfy some of those who were part of the Assembly because he had written in the *Annotations* that he did this in order to avoid slander and not because there was written evidence. Vitoria's response was that Erasmus's text "must be removed or revised."[64] Vitoria's concern was not necessarily with what Erasmus had written but that the text could leave "the reader doubtful."[65] Vitoria's stance, then, is not

---

62. Homza, "Erasmus," 78. I am in debted to Homza for the following material concerning Vitoria and Erasmus.

63. Ibid., 82.

64. Ibid., 92.

65. Ibid.

against Erasmus. Instead, he is interested in the catechesis and formation of the believer.

The second accusation that was entertained was Erasmus's comment "that only the Father was called true God in the Gospel."[66] At issue is the question of whether or not Erasmus was teaching that Christ was also God and what he meant by "Gospel." If he denied that Christ was truly God, then he would be going against Catholic teaching and the history of Christian thought, thereby positioning himself as a heretic. Furthermore, if "Gospel" is understood to include the Pauline corpus and the remaining part of the New Testament, then he would also be denying the divinity of Christ, which would also categorize him as a heretic. Following Vitoria's lead, the Assembly concluded that if Erasmus was being literal when he stated that the Gospel spoke of the Father as true God only, then this could be acceptable. Likewise, if he understood Gospel as the first four books of the New Testament, then Erasmus could be tolerated.[67]

Fear of the plague caused the Assembly to disband without drawing conclusions, and the Inquisitor General Manrique did not ask them to reconvene. What is important for our purposes is the interaction between the Spaniards and humanism. Erasmus becomes an important figure because he is representative of humanism, if not its prince and champion.

To reach a general understanding of the role of humanism in Spain we are faced with the obstacle of mis-categorization. In 1937 Marcel Bataillon published his *Erasme et l'Espagne*[68] in which he "identified Erasmus's supporters as progressives and labeled them as humanists."[69] The difficulty with these designations is that we know Vitoria is not a humanist in the same vein as Erasmus, but this does not necessarily imply that he did not support Erasmus. Even more, Bataillon juxtaposes progressives with "regressive factions," which leads one to believe that unless the Spanish theologians fully sided with Erasmus they would fall under the latter category.

This chapter does not attempt to prove that Vitoria was a humanist. He was not. I do, however, attempt to demonstrate that Spain has a rich history of humanism and that, at the very least, Vitoria was exposed to humanism. This contact with humanism could have allowed Vitoria to adopt humanistic techniques and concerns. With these possibilities available we

66. Ibid., 98.

67. Ibid..

68. Bataillon, *Erasmo*, 1950.

69. Homza, "Erasmus," 79.

should not be surprised should Vitoria have some of the same concerns as other humanists. Furthermore, realizing that rhetoric can also be viewed as a philosophy, the implementation of this philosophy by a theologian becomes more palatable. We are now in the position to demonstrate how Vitoria could have adopted rhetoric as a philosophy, which is identified with the humanist tradition, to address his concerns with the New World and the cruel treatment of the natives.

Conclusion

AT THE BEGINNING OF this project I set out to situate Francisco Vitoria within the discipline of theology as an individual who was concerned with, and became involved in, social justice issues, albeit from the confines of the Ivory Tower. While there are some legal and political science scholars who recognize the importance of Vitoria both within the history of Western thought and also as a contemporary figure, many fail to acknowledge the profundity and depth of Vitoria's thought. Within the study of religion, unfortunately, his works are rarely addressed, and when they are, they are usually seen in an unfavorable light. This inauspicious assessment is often the result of failing to consider Vitoria's works within his own context. In short, Vitoria is assessed based on contemporary values, which would be unproblematic if only his works were contextualized and understood in their entirety. Even some of his contempories have misunderstood Vitoria's overall contributions. Moreover, even scholars living in advanced nations have failed to grasp Vitoria's robust arguments and thought. Those scholars who do give attention to Vitoria do so by contrasting him and his corpus to the works of Bartolomé de Las Casas—even though Vitoria's rational and systematic approach to the cruelties of the New World is quite different to the polemical style of Las Casas.

This book has demonstrated that Vitoria was a scholar whose works cross disciplines. He was willing to glean from various thinkers and disciplines in order to address his concerns, which some have centered on human rights, such as property rights, the right to self-govern, the right and freedom to adhere to a religious belief, as well as the basic right to survive and flourish. Vitoria was a scholastic theologian who employed humanistic approaches to compel change in the human being. As a scholar who made use of a variety of disciplines, his was a functional approach to the realities of the political affairs that he faced, and he addressed his social concerns from a theological perspective, even while never traveling to the new world. To be concerned with social issues demands the use of reason and rational arguments as well as practical considerations. This is especially demonstrated in *De Los Indios* and the development of *ius gentium*. The difficulty, however, is that if one does not recognize his multi-pronged approach, one will fail to grasp the full force of his argument and will be prone to a misreading of the text. What we glean from Vitoria's style is that a theologian must be willing to learn from other disciplines and allow theology to engage them so that there is an encounter of mutual engagement. This is especially important because it addresses the human being and all her complexities as a social, political, and communal being.

The first chapter, "Law, Conquest and the New World," situated the historical context of Vitoria and the conquest of the New World. I demonstrated the legal background for understanding Vitoria's approach in *De Los Indios*. The conquest has a rich legal history that must be acknowledged. Similarly, it is essential to recognize the—almost radical—emphasis of Spain and Portugal in making certain that their endeavors were legal and just. Vitoria was able to appeal to the significant role of law to address the cruelties found in the New World by developing the notion of the law of the nations, which he then used to hold the emperor accountable.

The second chapter, "Political Prudence and a World Community," brought to the forefront Vitoria's text *De Los Indios*, and considered the arguments and concessions he makes. I pointed out that Vitoria makes the concession that Spain has the right to be in the New World. However, this concession, I argue, is nothing more than a reflection of the political reality that Vitoria faced. Spain is already in the New World at the time that he writes in 1537, and has no intention of abandoning the great wealth it has discovered. Therefore, I argue, in addition to this concession, Vitoria develops his notion of *ius gentium* and applies it to the political affairs he is addressing. By doing this, Vitoria holds the emperor accountable to ensure the humane treatment of the natives. Implicit, and at times explicit, is the claim that if the emperor fails to act according to the law of nations, then he fails to live according to the moral and religious character of being the Holy Roman Emperor. Essential to the argument is that Vitoria questions Spain's conquest and presence from within the academic environment. Of course, this gives hope to individuals who are less prone to public activism but are equally concerned with justice.

The third chapter, "Restraining Power in War," situated Vitoria's final *relección, On War*. To fully appreciate his argument, I focused on historical figures that would have influenced his approach to the question of war. Vitoria fits within the history of just war theory by acknowledging the necessity of war in defense of the common good. At the same time, however, Vitoria maintains that the war must be limited because of the nature of war, which is violent and cruel. Finally, I noted that Vitoria hints that the notion of just war may be found on both sides. This admission demands that one reconsider the reasons for going to war. As in the previous chapter, Vitoria uses his academic position to call into question and restrain Spain's power.

In "Theology, Authority, and Coercion," the fourth chapter, I suggested possibilities for Vitoria's adoption of a rhetorical approach that I referred to as safe criticism. Here, I argued that this rhetorical device was common, not only in his time period, but also throughout history, especially when an individual is addressing a coercive force such as an Emperor. This is especially important for Vitoria who did not have the security of being appointed as "Protector of the Indians," which was granted to Las Casas. The thrust of the argument is that this rhetorical approach was part of the milieu in which Vitoria found himself. Furthermore, I argued that Vitoria recognizes that the Emperor must be convinced to change his policies and laws that affect his newly expanded empire.

The fifth chapter, "Spain, Humanism, and Vitoria," provided a brief overview of the humanistic-scholastic debate of the sixteenth century. Humanists and scholastics were engaged in competing disciplines that were often exclusive of one another. In Spain, however, there was an attempt to glean from both modes of thinking. This was not an attempt to reconcile the disciplines, but an acknowledgement that humanism and scholasticism had beneficial aspects. This utilization of these disciplines is especially seen in Vitoria, who adopted the humanistic style that Ernesto Grassi refers to as philosophical rhetoric, and combines it with scholasticism to shape an approach that gives attention to the moral quality of the individual. Again, many individuals heard Vitoria's lectures in which he adopted this approach.

In this book I have argued against conclusions that are based on anti-Spanish sentiments tainted by what traditionally has been called the Black Legend, which is the general perception that the Spanish empire acted cruelly and viciously against the natives of the New World. It is argued that their cruelty was motivated by their greed for wealth and riches. The difficulty with this reading is that it ignores the many goods that can be attributed to Spain, its scholars, and its clergy.

In addition to being influenced by the Black Legend, many tend to read Vitoria incorrectly because they fail to take the context into account. In the case of Vitoria's work, *On the Indians*, they have arbitrarily picked various aspects of the work in order to prove their arguments. I contend, however, that the only correct way to read Vitoria's work is to understand the text as a whole, as it was originally presented in the sixteenth century. When considered as a whole, one recognizes that the *relección*'s form and content reflect the rhetorical devices that were commonly used among the humanists. Such devices assumed that the audience was intelligent and rational, and able to reach their own conclusions based on the evidence that was presented.

A key aspect of Vitoria's work that has long been recognized is *ius gentium*—the law of nations. The Law of Nations gives Spain the right to go to the New World and participate in the commerce with the natives. What has often been neglected, which I point out, is that while Spain is given certain rights and benefits under the Law of Nations, Vitoria is also able to hold the Spanish Emperor accountable. This law judges the emperor and his actions. In so doing, Vitoria establishes a foundation for holding Spain accountable. Through this he is able to defend the rights of the natives to live in peace.

On another level I have argued for a multi-disciplinary approach to theology. A theologian ought to use the tools developed and used in other disciplines to address contemporary problems facing the theologian. This theological approach is found in Vitoria's use of scholastic and humanistic tools, as well as those found within the legal discipline. In Vitoria we see a theologian at ease in his use of other disciplines to shape and formulate his own position. He not only adopts and synthesizes these disciplines, but moves beyond them, as reflected in the Neo-Scholastic method that Vitoria helped to establish.

Vitoria provides a model and a method for addressing political affairs. This approach must take into account various disciplines that provide insight into human existence. Human beings are political, social, and spiritual beings who are concerned with justice. The obstacle is that there are various notions of what justice entails. Harmful ideas of justice can be attended to through a multi-disciplinary approach that demands the right treatment of human beings. In the same way the natives needed a protector in the form of a firebrand, over the long term, the cause of justice also requires the careful thinking about justice that Francisco Vitoria's interdisciplinary approach brings. Through his inter-disciplinary approach Vitoria demonstrates what he described in his initial *relección* when he states, "The office and calling of a theologian is so wide, that no argument or controversy on any subject can be considered foreign to his profession."

Bibliography

Albaladejo Mayordomo, Tomás, Emilio del Río, and José Antonio Caballero López. *Quintiliano: Historia y Actualidad De La Retórica: Actas Del Congreso Internacional "Quintiliano: Historia y Actualidad De La Retórica : XIX Centenario De La Institutio Oratoria."* Colección Quintiliano De Retórica y Comunicación. Vol. 2. Logroño, Spain: Gobierno de La Rioja, Instituto de Estudios Riojanos, 1998.

Anuario De Estudios Americanos. Seville: Escuela de Estudios Hispano-Americanos de la Universidad de Sevilla, 1944.

Aquinas, Thomas. *St. Thomas Aquinas on Politics and Ethics: A New Translation, Backgrounds, Interpretations.* Edited by Paul E. Sigmund. New York: Norton, 1988.

———. *Summa Theologica.* Edited by Craig Paterson. Translated by the English Dominican Friars. Viewforth Great Books. 2nd ed. Los Angeles: Viewforth, 2012.

Augustine. *Augustine: Political Writings.* Edited by Michael W. Tkacz et al. Indianapolis: Hackett, 1994.

———. *The City of God Against the Pagans.* Translated by R. W. Dyson. Cambridge Texts in the History of Political Thought. New York: Cambridge University Press, 1998.

Bakewell, P. J. *A History of Latin America: C. 1450 to the Present.* Blackwell History of the World. 2nd ed. Malden, MA: Blackwell, 2004.

Baldwin, John W. *The Scholastic Culture of the Middle Ages, 1000–1300.* Civilization and Society. Lexington, MA: Heath, 1971.

Bataillon, Marcel. *Erasmo y Espana: Estudios sobre la historia espiritual del siglo XVI.* Translated by Antonio Alatorre. Madrid: Fondo de Cultura Economica, 1950.

———. *Estudios Sobre Bartolomé De Las Casas.* Historia, Ciencia, Sociedad 127. Barcelona: Península, 1976.

Berman, Harold J. *The Interaction of Law and Religion.* Nashville: Abingdon, 1974.

———. *Law and Revolution: The Formation of the Western Legal Tradition.* Cambridge, MA: Harvard University Press, 1983.

———. *Law and Revolution II: The Impact of the Protestant Reformations on the Western Legal Tradition.* Cambridge, MA: Belknap, 2003.

Bloom, Harold. *Cervantes' Don Quixote.* Modern Critical Interpretations. Philadelphia: Chelsea, 2001.

Bono, Dianne M. *Cultural Diffusion of Spanish Humanism in New Spain.* New York: Peter Lang, 1991.

Boruchoff, David A. *Isabel La Católica, Queen of Castile: Critical Essays*. New Middle Ages. New York: Palgrave Macmillan, 2003.

Bouwsma, William J. *The Waning of the Renaissance, 1550–1640*. Yale Intellectual History of the West. New Haven, CT: Yale University Press, 2000.

Bright, David A., and Jane Goodman-Delahunty. "Gruesome Evidence and Emotion: Anger, Blame, and Jury Decision-Making." *Law and Human Behavior* 30/2 (April 2006) 183–202.

Brooke, Christopher Nugent Lawrence. *The Medieval Idea of Marriage*. Oxford: Oxford University Press, 1989.

Bundy, Murray Wright. *The Theory of Imagination in Classical and Mediaeval Thought*. University of Illinois Studies in Language and Literature 12. Urbana: The University of Illinois, 1927.

Burns, J. H. *The Cambridge History of Medieval Political Thought c. 350–c. 1450*. Cambridge: Cambridge University Press, 1988.

Burrus, Ernest J. "Alonso De La Vera Cruz († 1584), Pioneer Defender of the American Indians." *The Catholic Historical Review* 70/4 (October 1984) 531–46.

Calboli, Gualtiero, and Lucia Calboli Montefusco. *Quintiliano y Su Escuela*. Colección Quintiliano De Retórica y Comunicación 5. Logroño, Spain: Ayuntamiento de Calahorra, 2001.

Camillo, Ottavio Di. "Interpretations of Humanism in Recent Spanish Renaissance Studies." *Renaissance Quarterly* 50/4 (Winter 1997) 1190–1201.

Carbia, Romulo. *Historia de la Leyenda Negra Hispanoamericana*. Madrid: Consejo de Hispanidad, 1944.

Carlson, John D., and Erik C. Owens. *The Sacred and the Sovereign: Religion and International Politics*. Washington DC: Georgetown University Press, 2003.

Carrasco, David. "The Hermeneutics of Conquest." *History of Religions* 28/2 (November 1988) 151–60.

———. *Quetzalcoatl and the Irony of Empire: Myths and Prophecies in the Aztec Tradition*. Chicago: University of Chicago Press, 1982.

Casas, Bartolomé de las. *The Devastation of the Indies: A Brief Account*. Baltimore: The Johns Hopkins University Press, 1992.

Casas, Bartolomé de las, and Manuel Ballesteros Gaibrois. *Brevísima Relación De La Destrucción De Indias*. Publicaciones De La Fundación Universitaria Española. Vol. 2. Madrid: Fundación Universitaria Española, 1977.

Casas, Bartolomé de las, Hans Magnus Enzensberger, and Michel van Nieuwstadt. *The Devastation of the Indies; a Brief Account*. New York: Seabury, 1974.

Casas, Bartolomé de las, and Stafford Poole. *In Defense of the Indians; the Defense of the most Reverend Lord, Don Fray Bartolomé De Las Casas, of the Order of Preachers, Late Bishop of Chiapa, Against the Persecutors and Slanderers of the Peoples of the New World Discovered Across the Seas*. DeKalb: Northern Illinois University Press, 1974.

Cassirer, Ernst, Paul Oskar Kristeller, and John Herman Randall. *The Renaissance Philosophy of Man*. Chicago: University of Chicago Press, 1948.

Castañeda, Carlos E. "Fray Juan De Zumárraga and Indian Policy in New Spain." *The Americas* 5/3 (January 1949) 296–310.

Chauvet, Fidel de J. "Fray Juan De Zumárraga, Protector of the Indians." *The Americas* 5/3 (January 1949) 283–95.

Cicero, Marcus Tullius, Miriam T. Griffin, and E. M. Atkins. *On Duties*. Cambridge Texts in the History of Political Thought. Cambridge: Cambridge University Press, 1991.

Cicero, Marcus Tullius, Niall Rudd, J. G. F. Powell. *The Republic; and, the Laws*. Oxford World's Classics. Oxford: Oxford University Press, 1998.

Cicero, Marcus Tullius, and J. S. Watson. *Cicero on Oratory and Orators*. Landmarks in Rhetoric and Public Address. Carbondale: Southern Illinois University Press, 1986.

Cicero, Marcus Tullius, James E. G. Zetzel. *On the Commonwealth; and, on the Laws*. Cambridge Texts in the History of Political Thought. Cambridge: Cambridge University Press, 1999.

Compier, Don H., Pui-lan Kwok, and Joerg Rieger. *Empire and the Christian Tradition: New Readings of Classical Theologians*. Minneapolis: Fortress, 2007.

Cortés, Hernán, and Anthony Pagden. *Letters from Mexico*. New Haven, CT: Yale University Press, 1986.

Cover, Robert M., et al. *Narrative, Violence, and the Law: The Essays of Robert Cover*. Law, Meaning, and Violence. Ann Arbor: University of Michigan Press, 1992.

Crews, Daniel A. "Juan De Valdes and the Comunero Revolt: An Essay on Spanish Civic Humanism." *The Sixteenth Century Journal* 22/2 (Summer 1991) 233–52.

Cromwell, Oliver, and Wilbur Cortez Abbott. *The Writings and Speeches of Oliver Cromwell*. Cambridge, MA: Harvard University Press, 1947.

Davenport, Frances G., and Charles Oscar Paullin. *European Treaties Bearing on the History of the United States and its Dependencies*. Carnegie Institution of Washington 25. Papers of the Division of historical research 1–4. Washington DC: Carnegie Institution of Washington, 1937.

Durán, Diego. *Historia De Las Indias De Nueva España y Islas De La Tierra Firme*. Madrid: Banco Santander, 1991.

Durán, Diego, and Angel María Garibay K. *Historia De Las Indias De Nueve España e Islas De La Tierra Firme*. Biblioteca Porrúa 36–37. México City: Editorial Porrúa, 1967.

Dussel, Enrique. "Origen De La Filosofía Política Moderna: Las Casas, Vitoria y Suárez (1514–1617)." *Caribbean Studies* 33/2 (July–December 2005) 35–80.

———. *Resistencia y Esperanza: Historia Del Pueblo Cristiano En América Latina y El Caribe*. Colección Historia De La Iglesia y De La Teología. San José, Costa Rica: Cehila/D.E.I., 1995.

Dworkin, Ronald. *Sovereign Virtue: The Theory and Practice of Equality*. Cambridge, MA: Harvard University Press, 2000.

Earenfight, Theresa. *Queenship and Political Power in Medieval and Early Modern Spain*. Women and Gender in the Early Modern World. Burlington, VT: Ashgate, 2005.

Elshtain, Jean Bethke. *Augustine and the Limits of Politics*. Notre Dame: University of Notre Dame Press, 1995.

———. *Just War Theory*. Readings in Social and Political Theory. New York: New York University Press, 1992.

———. *Sovereignty: God, State, and Self*. Gifford Lectures. New York: Basic, 2008.

Erasmus, Desiderius, and Erika Rummel. *The Erasmus Reader*. Toronto: University of Toronto Press, 1990.

Fabié, Antonio María, et al. *Viajes Por España De Jorge De Einghen*. Libros De Ataño 8. Madrid: F. Fé, 1879.

Ferguson, Everett. *Backgrounds of Early Christianity*. 3rd ed. Grand Rapids: Eerdmans, 2003.

Fernandez Lopez, Jorge. "Rhetorical Theory in Sixteenth-Century Spain: A Critical Survey." *Rhetorica: A Journal of the History of Rhetoric* 20/2. (Spring 2002) 133–48.

Fernández-Santamaría, J. A. *The State, War and Peace: Spanish Political Thought in the Renaissance, 1516–1559.* Cambridge Studies in Early Modern History. Cambridge: Cambridge University Press, 1977.

Floyd, Troy S. *The Columbus Dynasty in the Caribbean, 1492–1526.* Albuquerque: University of New Mexico Press, 1973.

Francisca, and Gillian T. W. Ahlgren. *The Inquisition of Francisca: A Sixteenth-Century Visionary on Trial.* The Other Voice in Early Modern Europe. Chicago: University of Chicago Press, 2005.

Franklin, Julian H. *Jean Bodin and the Sixteenth-Century Revolution in the Methodology of Law and History.* New York: Columbia University Press, 1961.

Galindo Martín, Miguel Angel. *Cervantes y La Economía.* Colección Estudios 109. Cuenca: Ediciones de la Universidad de Castilla-La Mancha, 2007.

García Icazbalceta, Joaquín. *Don Fray Juan De Zumárraga.* México City: Andrade y Morales, 1881.

García Icazbalceta, Joaquín, and Rafael Aguayo Spencer. *Don Fray Juan De Zumárraga, Primer Obispo y Arzobispo De México.* Colección De Escritores Mexicanos 41–44. México City: Editorial Porrúa, 1947.

García Villoslada, Ricardo. *La Universidad De París Durante Los Estudios De Francisco De Vitoria.* Rome: Gregorian University, 1938.

García Villoslada, Ricardo, and Manuel Sotomayor. *Historia De La Iglesia En España.* Biblioteca De Autores Cristianos 16, 18, 21. Madrid: Edica, 1979.

Gibson, Charles. *The Black Legend: Anti-Spanish Attitudes in the Old World and the New.* New York: Knopf, 1971.

Giles, Mary E. *Women in the Inquisition: Spain and the New World.* Baltimore: Johns Hopkins University Press, 1999.

Golsan, Richard J. "Todorov's 'New' Humanism: France's 'Imperfect Garden.'" *South Central Review* 15/3–4 (1998) 47–53.

Gómez, Fernando. "Francisco De Vitoria in 1934, before and After." *MLN* 117/ 2 (March 2002) 365–405.

Gonzalez, Miguel Anxo Pena. *La Escuela de Salamanca.* Madrid: Biblioteca De Autores Cristianos, 2009.

Grassi, Ernesto. *Heidegger and the Question of Renaissance Humanism: Four Studies.* Medieval and Renaissance Texts and Studies 24. Binghamton, NY: Center for Medieval and Early Renaissance Studies, 1983.

———. *Rhetoric as Philosophy: The Humanist Tradition.* University Park: Pennsylvania State University Press, 1980.

Gratian, et al. *The Treatise on Laws: (Decretum DD. 1–20).* Studies in Medieval and Early Modern Canon Law 2. Washington DC: Catholic University of America Press, 1993.

Greenleaf, Richard E. "The Mexican Inquisition and the Indians: Sources for the Ethnohistorian." *The Americas* 34/3 (January 1978) 315–44.

Grewe, Wilhelm Georg, and Michael Byers. *The Epochs of International Law.* Berlin: de Gruyter, 2000.

Grotius, Hugo. *Of the Rights of War and Peace.* Holmes Beach, FL: Gaunt, 2001.

Gutiérrez, Gustavo. *Las Casas: In Search of the Poor of Jesus Christ.* Maryknoll, NY: Orbis, 1993.

Hamilton, Bernice. *Political Thought in Sixteenth-Century Spain.* Oxford: Clarendon, 1963.

Hanke, Lewis. *Aristotle and the American Indians: A Study in Race Prejudice in the Modern World*. Bloomington: Indiana University Press, 1970.

———. *History of Latin American Civilization: Sources and Interpretations*. Boston: Little, Brown, 1973.

———. *Las Casas and the Spanish Struggle for Justice in the Conquest of America*. Neue Zeitchrift Für Missionswissenschaft 22. New York: Institute of Latin American Studies, School of International Affairs, 1966.

———. *The Spanish Struggle for Justice in the Conquest of the America*. Dallas: Southern Methodist University Press, 1949.

Hanke, Lewis, and Bartolomé de las Casas. *All Mankind is One; a Study of the Disputation between Bartolomé De Las Casas and Juan Ginés De Sepúlveda in 1550 on the Intellectual and Religious Capacity of the American Indians*. DeKalb: Northern Illinois University Press, 1974.

Hartigan, Richard Shelly. "Francesco De Vitoria and Civilian Immunity." *Political Theory* 1/1 (February 1973) 79–91.

Herzog, Tamar. *Defining Nations: Immigrants and Citizens in Early Modern Spain and Spanish America*. New Haven, CT: Yale University Press, 2003.

Hobbes, Thomas, and Richard Tuck. *Leviathan*. Cambridge Texts in the History of Political Thought. Cambridge: Cambridge University Press, 1991.

Höffner, Joseph. *Christentum Und Menschenwürde, Das Anliegen Der Spanischen Kolonialethik Im Goldenen Zeitalter*. Trier: Paulinus, 1947.

———. *La Ética Colonial Española Del Siglo De Oro; Cristianismo y Dignidad Humana*. Madrid: Ediciones Cultura Hispánica, 1957.

Homza, Lu Ann. "Erasmus as Hero, or Heretic? Spanish Humanism and the Valladolid Assembly of 1527." *Renaissance Quarterly* 50/1 (Spring 1997) 78–118.

———. *Religious Authority in the Spanish Renaissance*. Johns Hopkins University Studies in Historical and Political Science, 118th ser., 1. Baltimore: Johns Hopkins University Press, 2000.

Huxley, G. L. "Aristotle, Las Casas and the American Indians." *Proceedings of the Royal Irish Academy. Section C: Archaeology, Celtic Studies, History, Linguistics, Literature* 80C (1980) 57–68.

Instituto Francisco de Vitoria. *El Caso De La "Barcelona Traction" Ante El Tribunal Internacional De Justicia*. Madrid: Instituto Francisco de Vitoria, 1971.

Jarrott, C. A. L. "Erasmus' Biblical Humanism." *Studies in the Renaissance* 17 (1970) 119–52.

Johnson, James Turner. "Aquinas and Luther on War and Peace: Sovereign Authority and the Use of Armed Force." *The Journal of Religious Ethics* 31/1 (Spring 2003) 3–20.

Jones, Serene. *Calvin and the Rhetoric of Piety*. Louisville: Westminster/John Knox, 1995.

Juderias, Julian. *La Leyenda Negra y La Verdad Historica*. Madrid: Bibl. y Museos, 1943.

Justenhoven, Heinz-Gerhard. *Francisco de Vitoria zu Krieg und Frieden*. Cologne: Bachem, 1991.

Justinian, Peter Birks, and Grant McLeod. *Justinian's Institutes*. London: Duckworth, 1987.

Kallendorf, Craig. *Humanist Educational Treatises*. The I Tatti Renaissance Library. Cambridge, MA: Harvard University Press, 2008.

Kamen, Henry. *The Spanish Inquisition: A Historical Revision*. New Haven, CT: Yale University Press, 1998.

———. "Toleration and Dissent in Sixteenth-Century Spain: The Alternative Tradition." *The Sixteenth Century Journal* 19/1 (Spring 1988) 3–23.

Kantorowicz, Ernst Hartwig. *The King's Two Bodies: A Study in Mediaeval Political Theology.* Princeton: Princeton University Press, 1997.

Keal, Paul. *European Conquest and the Rights of Indigenous Peoples: The Moral Backwardness of International Society.* New York: Cambridge University Press, 2003.

Kelley, Donald R. *Renaissance Humanism.* Twayne's Studies in Intellectual and Cultural History 2. Boston: Twayne, 1991.

Kraye, Jill. *The Cambridge Companion to Renaissance Humanism.* New York: Cambridge University Press, 1996.

Kristeller, Paul Oskar. *The Classics and Renaissance Thought.* Martin Classical Lectures 15. Cambridge, MA: Harvard University Press, 1955.

———. *Medieval Aspects of Renaissance Learning; Three Essays.* Duke Monographs in Medieval and Renaissance Studies 1. Durham, NC: Duke University Press, 1974.

———. *Renaissance Thought and the Arts: Collected Essays.* Princeton: Princeton University Press, 1990.

Kristeller, Paul Oskar, and Michael Mooney. *Renaissance Thought and Its Sources.* New York: Columbia University Press, 1979.

Kroef, Justus M. van der. "Francisco De Vitoria and the Nature of Colonial Policy." *The Catholic Historical Review* 35/2 (July 1949) 129–62.

Kwok, Pui-lan. *Postcolonial Imagination and Feminist Theology.* Louisville: Westminster John Knox, 2005.

Landa, Diego de, and Miguel Rivera. *Relación De Las Cosas De Yucatán.* Biblioteca Americana 10. Madrid: Historia 16, 1992.

Leibell, J. F. "The Church and Humanism." *The Catholic Historical Review* 10/3 (October 1924) 331–52.

Leinsle, Ulrich Gottfried. *Introduction to Scholastic Theology.* Washington DC: Catholic University of America Press, 2010.

Lerner, Ralph. *Playing the Fool: Subversive Laughter in Troubled Times.* Chicago: University of Chicago Press, 2009.

Liere, Katherine Elliot van. "After Nebrija: Academic Reformers and the Teaching of Latin in Sixteenth-Century Salamanca." *The Sixteenth Century Journal* 34/4 (Winter 2003) 1065–105.

———. "Vitoria, Cajetan, and the Conciliarists." *Journal of the History of Ideas* 58/4 (October 1997) 597–616.

Liss, Peggy K. *Isabel the Queen: Life and Times.* New York: Oxford University Press, 1992.

López de Palacios Rubios, Juan, Agustín Millares Carlo, and Matías Paz. *De Las Islas Del Mar Océano* [Insularum mari's oceani tractatus]. México City: Fondo de Cultura Económica, 1954.

López de Palacios, Juan. *Requerimiento de la Monarquía Española.* 1513. http://www.ciudadseva.com/textos/otros/requerimiento.htm.

Losada, Angel, Juan Ginés de Sepúlveda, and Bartolomé de las Casas. *Apología: [De Juan Ginés De Sepúlveda Contra Fray Bartolomé De Las Casas y De Fray Bartolomé De Las Casas Contra Juan Ginés De Sepúlveda].* Madrid: Editora Nacional, 1975.

Lowney, Chris. *A Vanished World: Medieval Spain's Golden Age of Enlightenment.* New York: Free Press, 2005.

Lugo, Luis E. *Sovereignty at the Crossroads? Morality and International Politics in the Post-Cold War Era.* Lanham, MD: Rowman & Littlefield, 1996.

Lupher, David A. *Romans in a New World: Classical Models in Sixteenth-Century Spanish America*. History, Languages, and Cultures of the Spanish and Portuguese Worlds. Ann Arbor: University of Michigan Press, 2003.

Maclean, Ian. *Interpretation and Meaning in the Renaissance: The Case of Law*. Ideas in Context. Cambridge: Cambridge University Press, 1992.

Madden, Marie Regina. *Political Theory and Law in Medieval Spain*. New York: Fordham University press, 1930.

Mancing, Howard. *Cervantes'* Don Quixote: *A Reference Guide*. Greenwood Guides to Multicultural Literature. Westport, CT: Greenwood, 2006.

Mathes, W. Michael. "Humanism in Sixteenth- and Seventeenth-Century Libraries of New Spain." *The Catholic Historical Review* 82/3 (July 1996) 412–35.

McCarthy, Conor. *Love, Sex and Marriage in the Middle Ages: A Sourcebook*. New York: Routledge, 2004.

McGuire, Martin R. P. "Mediaeval Humanism." *The Catholic Historical Review* 38/4 (January 1953) 397–409.

McKenna, Charles H. "Francisco De Vitoria: Father of International Law." *Studies: An Irish Quarterly Review* 21/84 (December 1932) 635–48.

Mendieta, Eduardo. *Latin American Philosophy: Currents, Issues, Debates*. Bloomington: Indiana University Press, 2003.

Menéndez Pidal, Ramón. *El P. Las Casas y Vitoria, Con Otros Temas De Los Siglos XVI y XVII*. Colección Austral 1286. Madrid: Espasa-Calpe, 1958.

———. *El Padre Las Casas y La Leyenda Negra*. Madrid: Consejo Superior de Investigaciones Científicas, 1962.

Montaigne, Michel de. *Montaigne's Essays and Selected Writings: A Bilingual Edition*. Edited and translated by Donald Murdoch Frame. New York: St. Martin's, 1963.

Muldoon, James. *Canon Law, the Expansion of Europe, and World Order*. Variorum 612. Aldershot: Ashgate, 1998.

———. *The Expansion of Europe: The First Phase*. Middle Ages. Philadelphia: University of Pennsylvania Press, 1977.

———. "Francisco De Vitoria and Humanitarian Intervention." *Journal of Military Ethics* 5/2 (2006) 128–43.

———. *Popes, Lawyers, and Infidels: The Church and The Non-Christian World, 1250–1550*. Philadelphia: University of Pennsylvania Press, 1979.

Nardin, Terry. *The Ethics of War and Peace: Religious and Secular Perspectives*. Ethikon. Princeton: Princeton University Press, 1996.

Nauert, Charles G., Jr. "The Clash of Humanists and Scholastics: An Approach to Pre-Reformation Controversies." *Sixteenth Century Journal* 4/1 (April 1973) 1–18.

———. "Humanism as Method: Roots of Conflict with the Scholastics." *The Sixteenth Century Journal* 29/2 (Summer 1998) 427–38.

Nebrija, Antonio de. *Gramatica de la Lengua Castellana*. Barcelona: Red Ediciones, 2004.

Nervo, Jean Baptiste Rosario Gonzalve de. *Isabella the Catholic, Queen of Spain: Her Life, Reign, and Times, 1451–1504*. Translated by T. West Temple. London: Smith, Elder, 1897.

Nicholas, Barry. *An Introduction to Roman Law*. Clarendon Law. Oxford: Clarendon, 1962.

Nunez Gonzalez, J. M. *El ciceronianismo en Espana*. Valladolid: Universidad de Calladolid, 1993.

Oberman, Heiko Augustinus. *The Dawn of the Reformation: Essays in Late Medieval and Early Reformation Thought.* Grand Rapids: Eerdmans, 1992.

———. *Luther: Man between God and the Devil.* New Haven, CT: Yale University Press, 1989.

O'Donovan, Oliver. *The Desire of the Nations: Rediscovering the Roots of Political Theology.* Cambridge: Cambridge University Press, 1996.

O'Meara, T. F. "The Dominican School of Salamanca and the Spanish Conquest of America: Some Bibliographic Notes." *The Thomist* 56 (1992) 555–82.

———. "The School of Thomism at Salamanca and the Presence of Grace in the Americas." *Angelicum* 71/3 (1994) 321–70.

Oost, Stewart Irvin. "The Fetial Law and the Outbreak of the Jugurthine War." *The American Journal of Philology* 75/2 (1954) 147–59.

Ozment, Steven E. *The Age of Reform (1250–1550): An Intellectual and Religious History of Late Medieval and Reformation Europe.* New Haven, CT: Yale University Press, 1980.

———. *The Reformation in the Cities: The Appeal of Protestantism to Sixteenth-Century Germany and Switzerland.* New Haven, CT: Yale University Press, 1975.

———. *Religion and Culture in the Renaissance and Reformation.* Sixteenth Century Essays and Studies 11. Kirksville, MO: Sixteenth Century Journal Publishers, 1989.

Pagden, Anthony. *The Fall of Natural Man: The American Indian and the Origins of Comparative Ethnology.* Cambridge: Cambridge University Press, 1986.

———. "The 'School of Salamanca' and the Affair of the Indies." *History of Universities* 1 (1981) 71–112.

———. *Spanish Imperialism and the Political Imagination: Studies in European and Spanish-American Social and PoliticalTtheory 1513–1830.* New Haven, CT: Yale University Press, 1998.

Peck, Douglas T. "Revival of the Spanish "Black Legend": The American Repudiation of Their Spanish Heritage." *Revista De Historia De América* 128 (January–June 2001) 25–39.

Pérez, Joseph, and Marcel Bataillon. *España y América En Una Perspectiva Humanista: Homenaje a Marcel Bataillon.* Collection De La Casa De Velázquez 62. Madrid: Casa de Velázquez, 1998.

Petrarca, Francesco, and Thomas Campbell. *The Sonnets, Triumphs, and Other Poems of Petrarch.* London: G. Bell, 1901.

Phillipson, Coleman. "Franciscus a Victoria (1480–1546). International Law and War." *Journal of the Society of Comparative Legislation* 15/2 (1915) 175–97.

Philpott, Dan. "Sovereignty." *The Stanford Encyclopedia of Philosophy* (Summer 2010). http://plato.stanford.edu/archives/sum2010/entries/sovereignty/.

Prescott, William Hickling, and James Lockhart. *History of the Conquest of Mexico.* New York: Modern Library, 2001.

Queraltó Moreno, Ramón-Jesús. *El Pensamiento Filosófico-Político De Bartolomé De Las Casas.* Publicaciones De La Escuela De Estudios Hispano-Americanos De Sevilla 233. Sevilla: Escuela de Estudios Hispano-Americanos, 1976.

Quintilian, and Harold Edgeworth Butler. *The Institutio Oratoria of Quintilian.* Loeb Classical Library. Cambridge, MA: Harvard University Press, 1936.

Ramos Pérez, Demetrio. *La Etica En La Conquista De America: Francisco De Vitoria y La Escuela De Salamanca.* Corpus Hispanorum De Pace 25. Madrid: Consejo Superior de Investigaciones Científicas, 1984.

Real Academia de la Historia. "Colección De Documentos Inéditos Para La Historia De España." Madrid: Academia de la Historia, 1842, 1895.

Reichberg, Gregory M., Henrik Syse, and Endre Begby. *The Ethics of War: Classic and Contemporary Readings*. Malden, MA: Blackwell, 2006.

Renaudet, A. *Préréforme et humanisme à Paris Pendant les premières guerres d' Italie (1494–1517)*. Paris: Librarie Ancienne Honore Champion, 1916.

Restall, Matthew. *Seven Myths of the Spanish Conquest*. Oxford: Oxford University Press, 2003.

Rivera-Pagán, Luis N. *A Violent Evangelism: The Political and Religious Conquest of the Americas*. Louisville: Westminster/John Knox, 1992.

Root, Deborah. "The Imperial Signifier: Todorov and the Conquest of Mexico." *Cultural Critique* 9 (Spring 1988) 197–219.

Rummel, Erika. *Biblical Humanism and Scholasticism in the Age of Erasmus*. Brill's Companions to the Christian Tradition 9. Leiden: Brill, 2008.

———. *Erasmus and His Catholic Critics*. Bibliotheca Humanistica and Reformatorica 45. Nieuwkoop: De Graaf, 1989.

———. *Erasmus as a Translator of the Classics*. Erasmus Studies 7. Toronto: University of Toronto Press, 1985.

———. "Et Cum Theolog Bella Poeta Gerit: The Conflict Between Humanists and Scholastics Revisted." *Sixteenth Century Journal* 23/4 (Winter 1992) 713–26.

———. *The Humanist-Scholastic Debate in the Renaissance and Reformation*. Harvard Historical Studies 120. Cambridge, MA: Harvard University Press, 1995.

———. *Jiménez De Cisneros: On the Threshold of Spain's Golden Age*. Renaissance Masters 3. Tempe: Arizona Center for Medieval and Renaissance Studies, 1999.

Saranyana, José Ignacio, and Carmen José Alejos-Grau. *Teología En América Latina*. Frankfurt: Vervuert, 2008.

Schevill, Rudolph. "Erasmus and Spain." *Hispanic Review* 7/2 (April 1939) 93–116.

Schwartz, Daniel. *Interpreting Suárez: Critical Essays*. Cambridge: Cambridge University Press, 2012.

Scott, James Brown. *The Spanish Origin of International Law: Lectures on Francisco De Vitoria (1480–1546) and Francisco Suarez (1548–1617)*. Washington DC: The School of Foreign Service, Georgetown University, 1928.

Scott, James Brown, and Francisco de Vitoria. *The Spanish Origin of International Law: Francisco De Vitoria and His Law of Nations*. Union, NJ: Lawbook Exchange, 2000.

Scott, S. P., Robert Ignatius Burns, and Alfonso. *Las Siete Partidas*. Middle Ages. Philadelphia: University of Pennsylvania Press, 2001.

Sotomayor, Manuel, Teodoro González García, and Pablo López de Osaba. *La Iglesia En La España Romana y Visigoda (Siglos I-VIII)*. Historia De La Iglesia En España 1. Madrid: Edica, 1979.

Spain, Charles, et al. *The New Laws of the Indies for the Good Treatment and Preservation of the Indians*. London: Chiswick, 1893.

Swift, Louis J. *The Early Fathers on War and Military Service*. Message of the Fathers of the Church 19. Wilmington, DE: Glazier, 1983.

Thomas, Hugh. *The Golden Age: The Spanish Empire of Charles V*. New York: Allen Lane, 2010.

———. *Rivers of Gold: The Rise of the Spanish Empire, from Columbus to Magellan*. New York: Random House, 2003.

Tierney, Brian. *Church Law and Constitutional Thought in the Middle Ages.* Variorum Reprint CS90. London: Variorum, 1979.

———. *The Crisis of Church and State, 1050–1300.* Englewood Cliffs, NJ: Prentice-Hall, 1964.

———. *The Idea of Natural Rights: Studies on Natural Rights, Natural Law, and Church Law, 1150–1625.* Emory University Studies in Law and Religion 5. Atlanta: Scholars, 1997.

———. *Natural Rights: Before Columbus and After.* Maurice and Muriel Fulton Lecture Series. Chicago: University of Chicago Press, 1995.

———. *Religion, Law, and the Growth of Constitutional Thought, 1150–1650.* Wiles Lectures 1979. Cambridge: Cambridge University Press, 1982.

———. "Vitoria and Suarez on *Ius Gentium*, Natural Law and Custom." Paper presented at The Nature of Customary Law: Philosophical, Historical, and Legal Perspectives conference, Cambridge, September 14–16, 2005.

Tierney, Brian, and Sidney Painter. *Western Europe in the Middle Ages, 300–1475.* 3rd ed. New York: Knopf, 1978.

Todorov, Tzvetan. *The Conquest of America: The Question of the Other.* New York: Harper & Row, 1983.

Townsend, Camilla. "Burying the White Gods: New Perspectives on the Conquest of Mexico." *The American Historical Review* 108/3 (June 2003) 659–87.

Trinkaus, Charles Edward. *In Our Image and Likeness: Humanity and Divinity in Italian Humanist Thought.* Ideas of Human Nature. Chicago: University of Chicago Press, 1970.

———. *The Poet as Philosopher: Petrarch and the Formation of Renaissance Consciousness.* New Haven, CT: Yale University Press, 1979.

———. *The Scope of Renaissance Humanism.* Ann Arbor: University of Michigan Press, 1983.

Villoslada, Ricardo G. *La Universidad de Paris Durante Los Estudios de Francisco de Vitoria O. P. (1507–1522).* Rome: Gregoriana University, 1938.

Vitoria, Francisco de. *Obras, Relecciones Teológicas.* Madrid: Biblioteca de Autores Cristianos, 1960.

Vitoria, Francisco de, and Vicente Beltrán de Heredia. *Comentarios a La Secunda Secundae De Santo Tomás.* Biblioteca De Teológos Españoles. Vol. nos. 2–3, 5–6, 17. Salamanca: S.N., 1932.

———. *Los Manuscritos de Maestro Fran Francisco de Vitoria, O.P.: Estudio Critico de Introduccion a Sus Lecturas y Relecciónes.* Biblioteca de Tomistas Espanoles 4, Madrid-Valencia: Santo Domingo el Real, 1928.

Vitoria, Francisco de, et al. *Reflection on Homicide and Commentary on* Summa Theologiae *IIa–IIae Q. 64 (Thomas Aquinas).* Mediaeval Philosophical Texts in Translation. Vol. 34. Milwaukee: Marquette University Press, 1997.

Vitoria, Francisco de, and Luis Frayle Delgado. *Sobre El Poder Civil; Sobre Los Indios; Sobre El Derecho De La Guerra.* Colección Clásicos Del Pensamiento 137. Madrid: Tecnos, 1998.

Vitoria, Francisco de, and Ramón Hernández. *Derechos Humanos En Francisco De Vitoria: Antología.* Biblioteca Dominicana 4. Salamanca: Editorial San Esteban, 1984.

Vitoria, Francisco de, Anthony Pagden, and Jeremy Lawrance. *Vitoria: Political Writings.* Cambridge Texts in the History of Political Thought. Cambridge: Cambridge

University Press, 1991. Watson, Alan. *The Digest of Justinian*. Philadelphia: University of Pennsylvania Press, 1998.

Vries, Hent de, and Lawrence Eugene Sullivan. *Political Theologies: Public Religions in a Post-Secular World*. New York: Fordham University Press, 2006.

Weaver, Muriel Porter. *The Aztecs, Maya, and their Predecessors: Archaeology of Mesoamerica*. Studies in Archeology. New York: Seminar, 1972.

Weissberger, Barbara F. *Isabel Rules: Constructing Queenship, Wielding Power*. Minneapolis: University of Minnesota Press, 2004.

————. *Queen Isabel I of Castile: Power, Patronage, Persona*. Colección Támesis 253. Rochester, NY: Tamesis, 2008.

Williams, Robert A., Jr. *The American Indian in Western Legal Thought: The Discourses of Conquest*. New York: Oxford University Press, 1990.

Winroth, Anders. *The Making of Gratian's Decretum*. Cambridge Studies in Medieval Life and Thought, 4th ser. 49. Cambridge: Cambridge University Press, 2000.

Witte, John. *From Sacrament to Contract: Marriage, Religion, and Law in the Western Tradition*. The Family, Religion, and Culture. Louisville: Westminster John Knox, 1997.

————. *God's Joust, God's Justice: Law and Religion in the Western Tradition*. Emory University Studies in Law and Religion. Grand Rapids: Eerdmans, 2006.

————. *Law and Protestantism: The Legal Teachings of the Lutheran Reformation*. Cambridge: Cambridge University Press, 2002.

————. *The Reformation of Rights: Law, Religion, and Human Rights in Early Modern Calvinism*. Cambridge: Cambridge University Press, 2007.

Witte, John, and Martin E. Marty. *Law and Protestantism: The Legal Teachings of the Lutheran Reformation*. Cambridge: Cambridge University Press, 2002.

Witte, John, and Johan David Van der Vyver. *Religious Human Rights in Global Perspective: Religious Perspectives*. Boston: Nijhoff, 1996.

Index